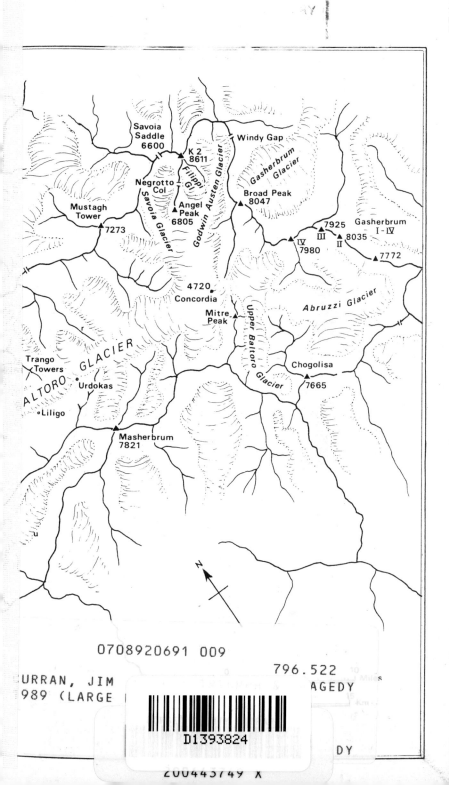

I've travelled the world twice over,
Met the famous: saints and sinners,
Poets and artists, kings and queens,
Old stars and hopeful beginners,
I've been where no-one's been before,
Learned secrets from writers and cooks
All with one library ticket
To the wonderful world of books.

K2, TRIUMPH AND TRAGEDY

K2 is the second highest mountain in the world. In the summer of 1986 there were nine expeditions on K2. The author was the only English-speaker at K2 Base Camp through the whole of that summer, first as a climbing cameraman with the unsuccessful British expedition and when that broke-up, he stayed on to support Al Rouse's attempt on the Abruzzi Ridge. This is his chronicle of the summer that twenty-seven climbers reached the summit, and also of the thirteen who died on K2, seven of them after reaching the summit.

JIM CURRAN

K2, TRIUMPH AND TRAGEDY

Complete and Unabridged

ULVERSCROFT
Leicester

First published in Great Britain in 1987 by
Hodder and Stoughton Ltd.,
London

First Large Print Edition
published October 1989
by arrangement with
Hodder and Stoughton Ltd.,
London

British Library CIP Data

Curran, Jim
 K2: triumph and tragedy.—Large print ed.—
Ulverscroft large print series: non-fiction
 1. Kashmir. K2. Mountaineering expeditions
 I. Title
 915.4′6

 ISBN 0-7089-2069-1

Published by
F. A. Thorpe (Publishing) Ltd.
Anstey, Leicestershire

Set by Rowland Phototypesetting Ltd.
Bury St. Edmunds, Suffolk
Printed and bound in Great Britain by
T. J. Press (Padstow) Ltd., Padstow, Cornwall

In memory of
Al Rouse and Nick Estcourt

Acknowledgements

MY thanks must go to many people for their kindness and help before, during and after the expedition, as well as to those who more directly enabled this book to be written.

I should like to thank Charles Williams, Marketing Director of Fuller, Smith and Turner PLC, for all his support in organising and sponsoring the British Fullers K2 expedition, and Anthony Smee who did so much to promote it; Shauna Falconer and Karen Rushworth for their hospitality and Gordon Hainsworth and Chris Slade who looked after our interests so well through the British Embassy in Islamabad.

At Bristol Polytechnic Neil Murison, Jeff Clements and Dr. Colin Chudley enabled me to take leave of absence, both for the expedition, and to write the book.

All the members of every expedition to

K2 in 1986 deserve my thanks, but in particular I must acknowledge the help given to me from Norman Dyhrenfurth, Goretta Casarotto, Michel Parmentier, Wanda Rutkiewicz, Michael Messner, Benoît Chamoux, Krystyna Palmowska, Janusz Majer, Peter Bozik, John Barry, Al Burgess, Phil Burke, Brian Hall and Dave Wilkinson.

For their assistance in the production of the book I must first and foremost thank Margaret Body, my editor, for her major contributions. Her constant encouragement, humour and criticism have been invaluable. Eva and Phil Curran spent long hours translating articles from Poland, as did Victoria Price the contributions from France. Rosie Smith had the unenviable job of typing the bulk of the manuscript and Roma Nall also helped out. Others who must be thanked are Chris Bonington, Geoff Birtles, Gemma and Becky Curran, Cass Lane, Audrey Salkeld, Jim Perrin, Terry Tullis, Charles Houston, H. Adams Carter, Pat Lewis, Bernard Newman and Josef Nyka. Finally thanks to Chris Lister, Allen Jewhurst, Barry Reynolds and Mark Stokes at

Chameleon Films who have worked so hard on the K2 film which is, at the time of writing, nearing completion.

For all these and to anyone I may have inadvertently left out, my most sincere thanks.

Jim Curran

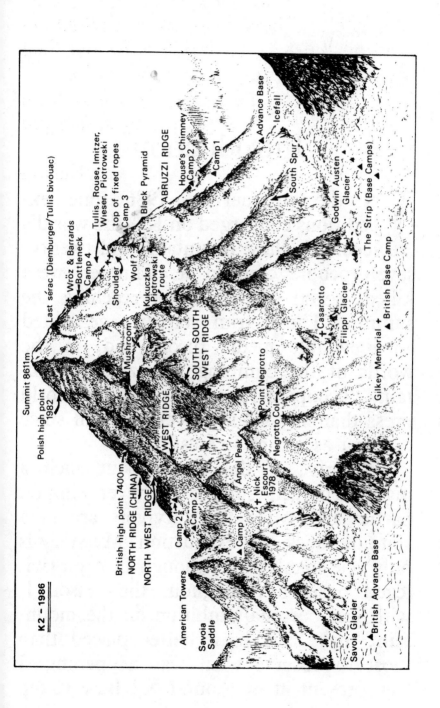

K2 – 1986

Summit 8611m

Polish high point 1982

Last sérac (Diemburger/Tullis bivouac)

Wröz & Barrards
Bottleneck
Camp 4

Tullis, Rouse, Imitzer,
Wieser, Piotrowski
top of fixed ropes
Camp 3

Black Pyramid

ABRUZZI RIDGE

House's Chimney
Camp 2

Camp 1

Advance Base
Icefall

South Spur

Godwin Austen
Glacier

Gilkey Memorial +

The Strip (Base Camps)

British Base Camp

Casarotto

Filippi Glacier

Shoulder

Mushroom

Wolf ?

Kukuczka
Piotrowski
route

SOUTH SOUTH
WEST RIDGE

WEST RIDGE

Point Negrotto

Negrotto Col

Angel Peak

Nick
Escourt
1978

British high point 7400m
NORTH RIDGE (CHINA)

NORTH WEST RIDGE

American Towers

Camp 2

Camp 1

Savoia Saddle

Savoia Glacier

British Advance Base

Introduction

IN the summer of 1986 nine expeditions converged on K2, the world's second highest mountain, and twenty-seven people climbed it. Thirteen were killed, seven of them after reaching the summit. These grim statistics generated an inevitable media furore and, in the words of the climbing magazine, *Mountain*, "occupied more space in the world press than any mountaineering event since the first ascent of Everest".

To arrive at the truth about such a highly charged subject is never simple, particularly when the survivors are in a state of shock and exhaustion. My story is only one man's view, though in my privileged position throughout the season I, with less personal ambition on the mountain, may have been better placed than most to observe what was happening. I was present at or around K2 Base Camp for the whole of the summer. As climbing cameraman with the British Fullers K2 expedition, my job initially was to film and report the activities of our own team while it was there. But as the summer passed, I became more and more drawn into the complex tapestry of events that unfolded, involving all the other expeditions and culminating in the final appalling storm and loss of five lives at or near Camp 4 at 7900 metres.

So this book is not a British expedition book. It is a look at what was happening on the mountain throughout the summer, at two outstanding new routes and an incredible twenty-three-hour ascent of the Abruzzi Ridge; at expeditions ranging from the massively supported Koreans to the dedicated soloist, Casarotto, whose story was one of the most poignant of the tragedies in a summer of tragedy. It is the story of a mountain which the experts still cannot decide the height of. Could it really be higher than Everest? It is an interesting speculation.

Whether it is the world's largest or second highest mountain, no one questions that K2 is the hardest and steepest, the challenge climbers take most pride in having overcome and in 1986 it took its toll of our ambitions.

As the climbing world first united in grief and shock, then fragmented in recrimination, I felt that I had to settle down and sort it all out in my own mind. It was a task I did not relish. I could be accused of setting myself up as judge and jury and even having an ego trip at the expense of the death of one of my best friends, Al Rouse. But the more I thought about it, the more conscious I became that I should first tell the story from my point of view and then, more difficult, try to analyse what went wrong. If nothing else it would perhaps set my mind at rest and also be a tribute to Al who always maintained a clinical and analytical approach to climbing controversies and would undoubtedly have been aghast at some of the conclusions being drawn from his own death.

Part One

The Mountain

1

DOWN, down, down, towards that distant spot of orange glowing in the night that meant food, drink, warmth and sleep. Stumbling, cursing, never-ending scree slopes, rucksack biting into aching shoulders. Still the faintest glimmer, the afterglow of sunset on the western skyline. A feeling of vast satisfaction and a rare fulfilment.

There were just three of us with Chepi, Andy's Peruvian girlfriend, making four as she anxiously watched the approaching pinpricks of light from our headtorches. We had just made the first ascent of Palomani Tranca, a mountain of 5633 metres straddling the borders of Peru and Bolivia, north of Lake Titicaca. For Geoff Tier and myself it was the end of a long journey and the high point of a friendship that had seen us through many climbs in Britain, an expedition to Barnaj II in the Kishtwar Himalaya in Northern India and the present outing to the Cordillera Apolobamba.

But even as I enjoyed our modest triumph the first faint rumbling of foreboding penetrated my mind as another much larger project loomed one step nearer. At some point I was going to have to make a decision about 1986. Two weeks later Geoff and I, with his fiancée Barbara and her friend Liz, walked the famous Inca Trail. It was a wonderful end to a light-hearted adventure. Yet in the quiet hours, walking alone from one Inca ruin to the next through spectacular and ever-changing mountain landscapes with the legendary ruined city of Machu Picchu getting nearer and nearer, my thoughts continually turned inwards.

Did I really want to go to K2 with Al Rouse and John Barry and burden myself yet again with the role of one-man film crew? I had no illusions that at forty-three I would be much use to the expedition in any other capacity. Peru had shown me that climbing within my own capacity, unencumbered by film-making responsibilities, could be vastly more enjoyable. Was there a real chance that Chris

Bonington would get a mini-trip organised to the Russian Caucasus to climb Mount Elbrus and perhaps even the beautiful twin-headed mountain Ushba? And if he did and I had the choice, which would it be? I hoped circumstances would conspire to make the decision for me. I knew which I would prefer. I had never been to Russia and, despite the chance of climbing on the world's second highest mountain, Pakistan and the Karakoram were familiar territory from two earlier trips. Already conflicts of self-interest, loyalty, friendships and ambition were jostling through my mind. Above all, I didn't want to have to tell Al or John that I wouldn't be going to K2.

In the event the choice *was* made for me. Chris Bonington's trip fell through and just before Christmas 1985 John and Al had confirmation from the Pakistani Ministry of Tourism that permission had been given for an expedition to attempt the unclimbed North-West Ridge of K2.

Al, one of my oldest and best friends, living just five minutes' walk away from me in the climber belt of suburban Nether Edge in Sheffield, was always reluctant to write me out of his plans, and any wavering on my part was met with a certain amount of light-hearted moral blackmail on his. Even so, for various reasons, practical, financial, even at times a real questioning of whether or not expeditions were worthwhile, I fluctuated wildly in my commitment until one evening in February when Al showed me a letter he had received expressing mild interest in a film from a production company in London I had never heard of. I suddenly realised how much I wanted to go.

Al had always been interested in K2, and his first visit to the mountain with Doug Scott in 1983 had fuelled what was to become a fixation. His satisfaction then at achieving his first 8000-metre summit, Broad Peak, was tempered by sorrow at the death of Dr. Peter Thexton high on the mountain, and frustration that on K2, the main objective of the expedition, they had barely scratched the surface. With Andy Parkin and Steve Sustad, Al had reconnoitred a new route, the South-South-East Spur, which is a variation (though quite a substantial one) on the Abruzzi Ridge, the route by which the mountain was first climbed in 1954. The Spur joins the Abruzzi at the Shoulder just below 8000 metres, then the route would follow the original line to the summit. Al's effort was little more than an acclimatisation foray and was abruptly halted not far up the Spur by an earthquake which dislodged colossal sérac avalanches all over K2 and the slopes of Broad Peak just opposite. Al described the earthquake as one of the most helplessly terrifying events he had ever experienced, for although the Spur was out of the direct line of the avalanches sweeping each side of it, he feared the enormous air displacements might drag them off to their deaths. Later on in the same expedition Doug Scott, Roger Baxter-Jones, Jean Afanassieff and Andy Parkin made a determined but unsuccessful attempt on the Spur, getting to within 200 metres of the Shoulder before retreating when Jean developed the symptoms of cerebral oedema.

These disappointments had made Al quite fanatical in his determination to do a new route on K2 and to do it alpine-style, with no porters, oxygen, fixed ropes or camps, moving continuously upwards, carrying everything on your back: food, fuel, climbing gear, tent and sleeping bag, just as one would in the Alps. At its purest there should be no previous attempts or foreknowledge of the climb, though this last is often impossible to adhere to in practice. Al's successful Himalayan ascents of Jannu, Nuptse and Broad Peak, and Kongur in China, had all been achieved alpine-style and he, with Doug Scott, was perhaps Britain's most vociferous apologist for the purist ethic. Al in particular was for ever questioning the validity of traditional siege climbs such as Annapurna South Face and Everest South-West Face, seeing them almost as evidence of the Decline and Fall of Western Civilisation. On the Mount Kongur expedition in 1981 he had frequently been at amiable logger-heads with Chris Bonington who, as leader of both these highly successful ventures, understandably defended them with some vehemence.

The still incomplete South-South-East Spur would have been an ideal objective for Al and he had applied to the Pakistani Ministry of Tourism with over eighteen months in hand for an attempt in 1986.

Originally, Al had planned a small six-man expedition and had asked me to go as cameraman and Base Camp Manager. Roger Baxter-Jones, Andy Parkin and possibly Jean Afanassieff were all pencilled into the original team but in the summer of 1985 came the shocking news that Roger, who had become a professional guide in Chamonix, had been killed with his client on the North Face of the Triolet. In 1983 Roger had almost made the first British ascent of K2, climbing to 8300 metres on the Abruzzi Ridge with a Spanish climber after the rest of the British team had returned home.

His loss was a major blow to the already dwindling ranks of top British Himalayan performers. Pete Boardman, Joe Tasker, Alex MacIntyre and Pete Thexton had all died within four years of each other. Then Andy Parkin had an appalling accident when an abseil piton failed and his survival hung in the balance for days. Miraculously his slow but continued recovery has finally enabled him to climb again. But Al's original team was no longer, and Al himself was faced with a set of changing priorities. His interest in mountaineering was never in doubt, but a combination of factors made his enthusiasm for K2 temporarily waver.

Undoubtedly the terrible succession of lost friends took its toll, though Al found it hard to express or admit it. But he had found a reawakening interest in British rock climbing. He discovered that even in his early thirties, he was not only still a first-class performer, but that hard rock gave him a satisfaction he had somehow lost or forgotten during the height of his expedition years. His precarious lifestyle of climber, writer, committee man, Vice-President of the British Mountaineering Council, lecturer and gentleman of leisure was always something of a balancing act and his constant "wheezes", as he called them, to achieve wealth through brilliant ideas but a minimum of work were usually doomed to failure. Inevitably he was more and more involved in the day to day necessity of earning a living: as equipment consultant to Berghaus, lecturing to clubs and societies in all corners of the country, writing countless articles for the climbing press. Yet Al was increasingly uncon- vinced that he wanted to go the way of the professional climber, epitomised by Chris Bonington. But the decision *not* to do so had never been made, let alone a satisfactory alternative discovered, and so it became imperative that expeditions like K2 should exist and, almost as important, be seen to exist, so that somehow he could still use his name and reputation to carry him through the next season of trade fairs, lectures, magazine articles and one-off commissions as guide, safety officer for films or whatever.

So Al hedged his bets. Without totally pulling out of K2 he offered the leadership to John Barry, the iconoclastic ex-Marine and former director of Plas y Brenin, the centre for outdoor pursuits in North Wales. Despite the frequent occasions when Al professed a growing disillusionment with expeditions, blaming them, with some cause, for the subsequent failure of emotional relationships, few close to him doubted that, in the event of permission being given for K2, he would be unable to say no. And so eventually it proved. Meanwhile John, himself in the middle of changing jobs and moving gradually from the protective embrace of an army career to the solitary insecurity of a self-employed writer, accepted the leadership of the still unconfirmed K2 expedition.

Perhaps because of the more than usual uncertainty surrounding the expedition it was difficult for the prospective members to put too much time and energy into its organisation. All were old hands at the expedition game, for by now it involved Brian Hall, Phil Burke, John Porter and the Burgess twins, Al and Aid. But there was nothing firm enough to get excited about, and with many other options available to most of them, it perhaps didn't matter enough whether K2 was on or off.

When permission finally *did* arrive it was not for the hoped-for South-South-East Spur but for the great unclimbed North-West Ridge which marks the frontier between Pakistan and China. The news put a very different complexion on the expedition, for it was highly unlikely that such a big and long route could be climbed in pure alpine-style and even Al's near-missionary zeal had to be tempered with realism. The record of previous attempts did nothing to alter that view.

The first, in 1975, was a large American expedition. It was led by Jim Whittaker and chronicled with great, and at times disturbingly personal, attention to every last detail of the vitriolic arguments that beset it by Galen Rowell in his book, *In the Throne Room of the Mountain Gods*. The expedition suffered from being the first one allowed to the mountain since 1960. The whole of the western end of the Karakoram, uncomfortably close to both India and China, had been closed for political reasons. When restrictions were at last lifted by the government of Pakistan in 1974 it was inevitable that a flood of expeditions would apply for what was seen as the biggest and best set of mountaineering objectives left in the world, with unclimbed mountains and new routes on the few that had been climbed providing an almost infinite number of possibilities.

Consequently the area was invaded by a mass of expeditions expecting and demanding the same sort of system of administration, transport and porterage that had taken years to evolve in Nepal where, in any case, far fewer expeditions are allowed in at any one time. Many expeditions failed even to reach their objectives and were ground down by porter strikes, desertions, thefts and misunderstandings of ill-thought-out regulations. The Americans had their fair share of these which conspired to pull the team apart. Half-beaten on their arrival at Base Camp, which in itself took many days to reach from Concordia following the desertion of most of the porters, they then compounded their problems by attempting to start the Ridge at the Savoia Saddle at the head of the Savoia Glacier. From here they hoped to bypass the first obstacle on the North-West Ridge. This is a series of pinnacles separated by knife-edged ridges, which they hoped to avoid by climbing a snow ramp running behind them on the northern (Chinese) side of the ridge.

The ramp, despite a previous aerial reconnaissance, proved to be non-existent and the pinnacles had to be tackled direct, giving difficult, intricate and time-consuming climbing. The route was wholly unsuitable for transporting loads along its convoluted crest and the expedition, whose problems were further compounded by almost constant bad weather and illness, eventually gave up before the traverse of the pinnacles was complete. Lack of time prevented any other options being taken up and the expedition was abandoned. Rowell's book, which also combines a history of K2 to that date and is a superb visual record of the Karakoram, remains a sad monument to the whole sorry saga.

The other attempt on the North-West Ridge was in 1982. The expedition was a large, somewhat improbable, combination of fifteen Poles and six Mexicans. They avoided the American Towers and gained the ridge beyond them by a hanging valley leading off the Savoia Glacier and the direct ascent of a steep ice face to a point just below 7000 metres. (Interestingly, this was the way first proposed on a reconnaissance in 1974 by veteran American mountaineers Bob Bates and H. Adams Carter.)

Like the Americans before them, they suffered continuously bad weather but eventually established camps and fixed rope up to 8100 metres. Late in the season, on 6th September, a summit attempt by Leszek Cichy and Wojciech Wröz was forced back at 8200 metres.

Wröz had also been on the Polish 1976 expedition to the North-East Ridge and on that occasion had been to within 200 metres of the summit. It seemed cruel luck for him to be turned back so close on each unclimbed route.

So the North-West Ridge remained unclimbed, if not unknown. It was a worthy, indeed major, Himalayan objective but it was not what we had originally wanted or expected. It immediately increased the estimated cost of the expedition, would demand a bigger team and, in all probability, a siege-style ascent with camps and fixed ropes. It would involve the team in a way of climbing that most of them to some degree or another had publicly stated they disapproved of, considered out of date and even pointless. Those that had had experience of fixed-rope expeditions (which were mainly those who had been on Everest with Al in 1980) had no fond memories of what it had entailed, with a never-ending treadmill of load-carrying and trail-breaking and little or no excitement of lead climbing. I was probably the only person to welcome the change of route wholeheartedly as it would be far easier for me to film on a fixed-rope attempt, and I would almost certainly get higher on the mountain than on an alpine-style ascent. But the chance of a new route on K2 doesn't happen every day and everyone (including Al) could rationalise their standpoint to accommodate the new circumstances. There even seemed to be an unspoken and irrational hope that the reality, once on the mountain, would be somehow different and better than expected.

The climbing team was increased to eight with the inclusion of Dave Wilkinson. He, with the minimum of fuss and publicity, had over the years become one of Britain's most accomplished and successful mountaineers, through his winter climbs in the Alps and on frequent small trips to the Karakoram and South America. Al's participation, of course, had never really been in doubt and Dr. Bev Holt and Jim Hargreaves were added as doctor and Base Camp Manager respectively.

Only one minor snag prevailed which was a total lack of financial backing. The months of uncertainty over our permission had made achieving sponsorship or media deals more than usually awkward, and the problem with K2, as others had found before us, is quite simply that it *is* the second highest mountain in the world, and advertising, promotion and production companies don't like second best. Al came up with "The World's Hardest Mountain" as a heading for our notepaper. I am always slightly wary of superlatives. K2, at 8611 metres, is arguably the most difficult and challenging of the world's fourteen 8000-metre peaks, but many other lower mountains are technically far harder, even if they don't have any of the problems of high altitude and all the logistical head-aches posed by a mountain as remote as K2. But "Hardest" it was, though, when sponsorship eventually materialised, it was for a rather different and unexpected reason but, strangely, still connected with notepaper.

John Barry had sent letters to a wide range of firms and the "we regret" replies were trickling back with depressing regularity. But one found its target. In his office at the Griffin Brewery, Chiswick, Fullers' Managing Director, Charles

Williams, was intrigued by John's home address—The Old Brewery, Llanrwst. This alone made him stop and read the rest of John's letter.

A few days later, with John now at a Trade Fair in the States, Al and I went down to London by train, clad in suits and ties and both horribly hung-over from the British Mountaineering Council bi-annual conference that had just finished in Buxton.

"Well, we may not look much like climbers," muttered Al as we hailed a taxi to take us from Hammersmith Broadway to Chiswick, "but at least it's obvious that we understand their product and endorse it personally."

When John returned, he and Al carried on the negotiations with Fullers and I concentrated on getting a film deal—by now an urgent priority for we had glibly assured Fullers that there would be both a documentary film and ITN news reports. Neither were confirmed until the very last minute, by which time I was on the verge of nervous exhaustion from so much brinkmanship.

I was certainly not alone. Al had by now

reverted to his original role as expedition leader, for the simple reason that he understood the expedition administration game, particularly in Pakistan, better than any of us. Al's problems were compounded by the knowledge that his girl-friend, Deborah, was in the early stages of pregnancy. The prospect of returning from K2 a father was one he found bewildering. The huge pressure of coping with so many diverse problems inside four months were really too much for one person to undertake. Al, who was more capable than most of carrying a mass of complex detail around in his head, found himself over-loaded with responsibilities. Brian, in charge of equipment, was similarly burdened, as was John Porter looking after food. Jim Hargreaves was given all the unglamorous jobs that no-one else could be bothered with and did an incredible job acquiring so many of the humdrum but indispensable items than an expedition relies on.

Al saw me as much as a friend and, to some extent, confidant, as he did a film-maker, for we had become close since 1981 when we both went with Chris Bonington to Mount Kongur in China. Al was a great believer in sticking to successful combinations and had a long-lasting loyalty to old climbing friends. He wanted me to come anyway, with or without a film. But I still felt I could only justify the trip if there was going to be a film. At the last minute we struck a deal with some old associates of former expeditions, Chameleon Films in Leeds. Chameleon had produced the film of Chris Bonington's tragic K2 West Ridge expedition in 1978, when Nick Estcourt, a close friend of ours, had been killed in an avalanche; Al's unsuccessful attempt on the West Ridge of Everest in the winter of 1980; and the Mount Kongur film in 1981. I never seriously imagined that K2 would appeal to them at all.

But realism has never been an obstacle to Chameleon Films and with a strong feeling of déjà-vu we started on the usual negotiations, based on incorrigible optimism (from them), long-suffering realism (from me) and delusions of grandeur (from Al). When we had all pulled the wool over each other's eyes to our mutual satisfaction we assumed a deal had been struck. My requests for good reliable gear and filmstock were met with looks of pained affront that I should even have to ask the question. I duly carted off all the odds and sods of equipment that over the years had proved their worth on rather too many trips. It would have to suffice.

Amidst all our preparations one thing cheered me up. The variety of personalities going to K2 reminded me of my first, and certainly happiest, expedition in 1976 to the Trango Tower with Joe Brown, Martin Boysen and Mo Anthoine. John Porter was heard to say after one expedition meeting which had degenerated into the inevitable drunken story-telling marathon in the pub, that if he was going to die on the trip, it would be of laughing. I hoped he was right (not dying of course, but laughing). Without being superstitious I have always trusted my feelings for trips: good vibes, as the old 'sixties phrase had it. That I felt this expedition would be a good one simply proves how such feelings are so much wishful thinking.

For economy's sake we were flying to Pakistan in two groups. On 29th April the first party assembled at Terminal 3,

Heathrow. With Al and me were John Barry, Jim Hargreaves and Al and Aid Burgess. After checking in we stood around in small self-conscious groups waiting for the last goodbyes. Deborah, and my girlfriend, Cass, had come to see us off.

A cleaning lady approached us. "Are you part of a group, dears? My hobby is autographs, I've had them all—footballers, politicians, pop groups, you name it—all sorts," she prattled merrily on until Al tried to answer her question. "Oh yes, climbers, I've had lots of those, though what you see in it I just don't know. Mind you, you normally lose one, don't you? But you always get a replacement for next year."

She produced a well-thumbed autograph book from her overalls and we all dutifully signed it, trying not to laugh, while Cass and Deborah looked on appalled.

The flight was called and it was time to go. A quick embrace through a blur of tears and a lump in the throat. Then we went our different ways, waving as we turned the corner into Passport Control.

"Strange for Cass to get so upset,"

mused Al as we wandered towards the Duty Free Shop. "Really, your chances of coming back are miles higher than mine."

Clutching our boarding cards, we stepped once more into the strange life and rituals of a mountaineering expedition, wondering as the 747 lifted off and turned in a big circle over Central London heading East to the Channel, what this one would bring.

2

AL had joked that there would be so many expeditions at K2 Base Camp that I would be able to make a film about all the other film-makers, but I hadn't paid much attention to him, assuming that the Rouse Factor was at work and, as usual, he was exaggerating. On this occasion, though, it was no more than the truth. Others were also preparing to leave for Pakistan. The smallest expedition already had. The Italians, Renato Casarotto, with his wife Goretta, and two strong Basque climbers, Mari Abrego and Josema Casimiro, were preparing to walk in to the mountain. Casarotto had plans to solo an ambitious unclimbed route, while Mari and Josema were to attempt the Abruzzi Ridge. Both men were experienced climbers who had been on the North Ridge of Everest and attempted K2 once before.

In Paris another small expedition, Maurice and Liliane Barrard and Michel

Parmentier were almost ready for departure. In Warsaw Wanda Rutkiewicz was about to join them.

The Ministry of Tourism had given permission for no less than nine expeditions to K2 alone. Why they had done this seemed something of a mystery, for it was almost inevitable that it would lead to all sorts of complications for all concerned, including the Ministry itself.

We wondered if it had any connection with a letter Al had earlier received from General Mirza, President of the Alpine Club of Pakistan, asking how many possible routes Al reckoned there were on K2, excluding those in China. Al had replied that there were nine, not of course imagining that nine expeditions should go to K2 at the same time. But not only had nine permissions been given but several were for the same route at the same time. No one had been given permission for the West Ridge or the unclimbed West Face, both major features. But the Poles, Americans, Italians and, separately, Casarotto, would be on the South-South-West Ridge, and Austrian, French and Korean teams would all be on the Abruzzi. Finally, the climbing impresario, Dr. Karl Herr-ligkoffer, was leading a joint German-Swiss party with permission for both Broad Peak and K2. It seemed a recipe for chaos but not one that should concern us unduly as we had the North-West Ridge to ourselves, and it was the route furthest away from all the others.

Perhaps the granting of so many permissions, not just for K2, but for Broad Peak, the Gasherbrum peaks and Chogolisa, had a political-public relations motive, apart from the more obvious financial one. The perennial dispute with India over the Kashmir border had flared up again with troop movements and fighting along the Siachen Glacier, east of K2. The hostilities were unofficial and had received little media coverage. (Al, who had theories about most things, came up with one that probably owed its origins to Evelyn Waugh's *Scoop*. This was that as there were no decent hotels in the area, journalists wouldn't go there, therefore the war didn't exist!) But the area was certainly troubled, which might explain the long delay in giving permission. If this was the case then they may have wanted to get as many foreign expeditions as possible into the area to demonstrate to India and the rest of the world that Pakistan had a firm grip on her territory.

On first glance, Rawalpindi and Islamabad seemed much the same as they had on my last visit in 1978. Then the disgraced ex-president Bhutto was languishing in Rawalpindi jail, waiting to be hanged. General Zia-ul-Haq had assumed power and the country was, if not in turmoil, certainly uneasy. Now, eight years later, it would be interesting to see what had changed. One thing that hadn't was the offices of the Ministry of Tourism. Here was the legacy of the British Raj epitomised in the stacks of ageing files of paperwork (all in triplicate), the limp fan on the ceiling blowing odd pieces of paper around the office and the staff, still as bewilderingly busy as ever, engaged in God only knows what mysterious bureaucratic tasks as they swept purposefully from the inner sanctum to the outer office, clutching bits of paper and talking loudly to their subordinates. I suppose it is much the same everywhere and an average British town hall is probably no different, but there is a quite Kafkaesque sense of never-ending purposelessness as one attempts to find out simple answers to straightforward questions. It's best never to ask any and always agree. The phone rings constantly and two conversations will be carried on simultaneously, half in English and half in Urdu, with frequent asides to harassed clerks. For a K2 expedition the whole ritual is even more complicated and we were treated to a no-holds-barred series of meetings of quite mind-numbing boredom. Mercifully at the beginning of May it was not intolerably hot, but it was still all too easy to nod off.

We had a week to get as much done as possible before the "second half" arrived. The first priority was to retrieve our freighted gear from the Customs shed at Islamabad airport. This involved hiring an agent who would speed the process up with a system of discreet bribery and cajolement of the many officials whose signature is needed on endless forms before the goods can be released. Al, knowing the score, and what he was in for, spent a day on his own at the airport, at the end of which the agent announced: "I am pleased to give you good news. The Customs Officer will be inspecting your luggage at two p.m. promptly. He will wish to see boxes number 15, 23, 34 and 72. If there is anything in those boxes that you do not wish him to see, I suggest you remove them immediately." It was comforting to know that some things in Pakistan would never change.

British expeditions have been incredibly fortunate as over the years a network of hospitality contacts has been maintained through the British Embassy. Other nationalities are not so fortunate. Many of them stay at Flashman's Hotel in Rawalpindi, another ornate remnant of the Raj that has seen better days. It was here that Al and I arranged to meet our Liaison Officer, Lieutenant Agha Hussein. He was only twenty-four years old and had no previous experience of mountaineering expeditions. He had volunteered to act as Liaison Officer for a trekking party but when our original man, a major, broke his leg, Agha had been drafted in at the last minute. He seemed terribly young for his age but very enthusiastic about the prospect of going to K2, and most anxious to see his personal kit, for this is one of the biggest perks. Some of it wasn't going to fit as, from the measurements that we had been sent, our major had been a well-fed one, and Agha was slim. Luckily his boots fitted, which was the most important thing. I thought Agha would be okay but Al wasn't so sure.

The week in Islamabad was not the opportunity I had hoped for to unwind and get psyched up for the expedition itself. All of us had our tensions, apart from the laid-back Burgess twins who could relax in almost any circumstances. The arrival of John Porter, Brian Hall, Dave Wilkinson, Bev Holt and Phil Burke meant more hands for the huge task of repacking everything into porter loads ready for the walk-in, it also meant more voices, more opinions and, inevitably, more friction.

It wasn't that we argued bitterly or that there was any ill-feeling. Quite the contrary, as we drank the evenings away in the agreeable company of our hosts in the British Embassy Club. But there was an underlying feeling that the eleven of us were not yet making up a team. Already there was too much point-scoring and criticism, rather than support and agreement. No-one was trying to, it just happened, and it forced people onto the defensive. We should have known better but it became a habit. Some of it stemmed from our own egos and inability to admit our deficiencies, some from Al's reluctance to lead from the front.

This was almost a matter of principle with him, for he always believed that leadership was unnecessary, just a word on a piece of paper to satisfy bureaucracy. But the fact was he didn't enjoy it and, because of that, wasn't very good at it. Al always saw himself very much as one of the lads and couldn't see any necessity to be otherwise, even when the situation demanded it.

Once more the team was going to split up. We had hired a bus to carry the gear up the Karakoram Highway to Skardu and John Porter, John Barry, Jim Hargreaves and I would travel with it, a two-day journey, while the others made the sixty-minute flight to Skardu on one of PIA's old but reliable Fokker Friendships. I looked forward to the drive as I wanted to film what I had been told was one of the great road-building feats in the world.

The day before we left we all went to the Ministry of Tourism to be briefed. The Ministry sets great store by this and insists on everyone being present and aware of all the regulations. As many of them are impossible to obey, and many others ignored by everyone and as I had already been through this twice previously, it was not my idea of fun and the only diversion occurred when a distraught couple, Maurice and Liliane Barrard, arrived from the airport in the middle of it all. They had left their entire expedition budget— thousands of dollars plus airline tickets and passports on the back seat of a taxi! A nightmare start to an expedition and one that could only deal a devastating blow to their morale.

It was during the briefing that I became aware of the sheer numbers of people going to K2. We were lucky to be setting out so early for it seemed almost certain that porter shortages would occur as the season got under way. From the briefing it struck me that even now, ten years after my first visit, the Ministry were as out of touch with reality as ever. A demand for the expedition to stay together at all times just couldn't be enforced and made the Liaison Officers' job impossible. The demand that the Liaison Officers were to be encouraged to climb was also absurd for it raised the hopes of totally inexperienced men to imagine that their army training would enable them to climb K2. Agha already had a fanatical gleam in his eye as he asked whether he would have the honour of being the first Pakistani army officer to climb K2. Not much point in disillusioning him so soon and, hoping the walk-in would sort him out, we avoided the question. But this year there would be not just one bored soldier at Base Camp, but nine! It was not difficult to see problems arising here as well.

After the departure of the others early next morning for the flight to Skardu we awaited the arrival of a highly ornate bus from Gilgit. The assembly of our two and a half tons of gear outside the British Club looked like an attempt on something from the *Guinness Book of Records*, for it was obvious to all of us, except Al, that it couldn't possibly be reaccommodated on the bus. But Al had done this more recently than the rest of us and to our utter amazement it somehow fitted in. As dusk fell we set off, crammed together on the front row of seats. The driver took a battered tape of shrill wailing music and slotted it into an ancient cassette, wired precariously to the dashboard. Carefully turning the volume up until maximum distortion was achieved, he lit an evil-smelling K2 cigarette and, at peace with the world, settled down to drive to the first stop, Allahabad.

Two days later the bus wound its way over the last miles of silvery desert ringed by snow-capped mountains to the distant lights of Skardu. I found the journey a slightly disappointing experience. The Karakoram Highway is indeed an incredible achievement but to my mind nowhere near as spectacular as roads I have travelled in Peru and India, or indeed the Highway itself from Kashgar in China to the Karakol Lakes. For it was from the other end of the same road that Al and I had driven to the foot of Mount Kongur in 1981; a strange thought as that had involved thousands of miles flying, via

Hong Kong, Peking and Urumchi to complete a journey that was only a few hundred miles north of where we now were.

It is not difficult to see why Baltistan is sometimes referred to as Little Tibet, for the great valley of the Indus that contains the capital Skardu does bear some resemblance to Lhasa and its surroundings. Here however there is no Potala or Bhuddist culture, but the mosque and the amplified wail of the Muezzin calling the Moslem faithful to prayer. Skardu is an unlovely place, apart from the ancient fort and the superb airy view of desert, river and hill. But the arrival of the Karakoram Highway has brought some prosperity to its bazaars and softened the grim frontier feel I remembered.

Like most expeditions, we stayed at the expensive but pleasant K2 Motel while we sorted out our gear yet again for the jeep drive to the roadhead at Dasso. The others were already ensconced and as we unloaded the bus Phil Burke told me, still wide-eyed at the memory, of the flight from Rawalpindi. The PIA pilot, knowing that there were climbers aboard, had circled around Nanga Parbat, to the consternation of those passengers who were not expecting it. Upon learning that he was flying the K2 expedition he said that if he had known he would have flown nearer to the Baltoro Glacier. Even so they had had a superb view of K2, Broad Peak and the Gasherbrum peaks on the horizon. Phil was mesmerised by K2 and described how it stood head and shoulders above its neighbours.

"I think we're going to have a real job climbing it," he finished dubiously.

In the courtyard of the K2 Motel piles of boxes and drums were growing. Amidst the chaos another truck arrived and disgorged the French expedition who had somehow managed to sort out their finances. The Barrards were a familiar name and Maurice and Liliane had chalked up quite a few major ascents between them. Maurice had climbed Hidden Peak and, with Liliane, both Gasherbrum II and Nanga Parbat. Michel Parmentier I had not heard of but the fourth member, Wanda Rutkiewicz, was the name to conjure with.

She had been the first European woman

to climb Everest and had also climbed Nanga Parbat. As they unloaded their gear I was impressed with the ease with which she carried heavy boxes, possessing a strength that was belied by her striking looks. I was forcibly reminded of Chris Bonington's concluding words in his book, *Quest for Adventure*, in which he attempts to find similarities in the people who have significantly contributed to the history of post-war adventure. "The keen-eyed adventurer gazing into the distance is maybe a cliché but it is also true. All the adventurers I met and interviewed had eyes that had a piercing, almost compulsive, quality. The other thing they had in common was the nature of their hands, strong capable hands very often large in proportion to their size." Wanda, with her almost archetypal Polish bone structure, wide cheekbones and strong jaw, fitted the description perfectly.

Maurice Barrard, tall and powerfully built, with longish prematurely grey hair, sideboards and moustache, reminded me of a sheriff in an old cowboy movie. I wouldn't have been surprised to see him in boots and spurs. Liliane was charming, coy and very French. She spoke no English but smiled a lot at everyone. And Michel Parmentier appeared to be the quintessential Frenchman, slightly built, his unruly dark curly hair normally covered with an English flat hat, sad brown eyes that lit up with good humour, and an expressive mouth, cigarette drooping from it. He spoke excellent English with a strong accent. He and Al hit it off straight away and I also enjoyed his infectious sense of the absurd. He had climbed Kangchenjunga in 1981 and worked as a war reporter for a Paris radio station in Beirut. Climbing 8000-metre peaks was obviously his idea of a holiday.

Before we had left Islamabad I had worked out a way of sending ITN news reports back to Britain. It was not a fool-proof system—nothing ever is in the East, but after our departure Al had changed it for no good reason. It didn't matter too much but I couldn't help feeling a bit resentful that he didn't seem to trust my judgement. Now, untidily sharing our last hotel room, trying to sort out our personal gear and a film box that could be easily got at during the walk-in, I felt more tense than ever. Al seemed terribly tired and absent-minded. Brian Hall had been violently sick and complained of a persistent headache. Before we left England I had joked that what the team needed was a psychiatrist, not a film-maker, and I began to wonder whether I was right. But John Barry had apparently shrugged off his early doubts and the twins, affable as ever, were jovially flirting with every female in the hotel. Dave Wilkinson was as usual eating as much as he could before the start of privation, Bev Holt was impressing on us the importance of preventative medicine and John Porter and Jim Hargreaves attempted to agree on the practicalities of food distribution from Skardu to Base Camp. The two could hardly have been more different, Jim the epitome of the army sergeant, and John the intellectual dreamer with his American 'sixties background that still evoked faint Woodstock echoes of love and peace. Jim's theory was that a childhood of alcoholic and chemically induced indulgences had caused John's mind to be attached to his body by only a stamp hinge. The nickname Stanley Gibbons soon followed, much to the bewilderment of John who, no philatelist, was unacquainted with the renowned London stamp dealers.

Another British expedition was stopping at the K2 Motel. Dai Lampard, who had two years previously narrowly failed to do an extremely hard new route on the Nameless Tower of the Trango Towers, had returned to attempt the huge West Face of Gasherbrum IV. With two expeditions snapping at our ankles Al became obsessed with the need to stay ahead of them. It would certainly pay us to get to the roadhead at Dasso first and sort out our 200 porters, but after that the carry to K2 Base Camp is charged at a set fee, based on a fourteen-day walk-in, including two rest days, so there's no financial incentive to sprint along.

But first we had to get the gear on tractors for the fifty-mile drive up to Dasso. Al and I had often tried to impress the others (for only Dave and Brian had visited the Karakoram before) with stories of the searing heat of the walk-in, and sunstroke on the jeep drive. But by the time we arrived at Dasso we were cold and shivering. The snowline was less than a thousand metres above us and it seemed that winter was still upon us in early May. Ahead the dark valley walls of the Braldu Gorge were etched with old snow. What would the going be like higher up?

The rest of the day was spent choosing porters and issuing them with the piles of coats and macs we had bought in the bazaars of Rawalpindi. Regulations insist on a plastic mac for everyone. Our purchases were cheap and good quality, having been originally intended, for some unfathomable reason, for famine relief. But they had been mysteriously diverted to the bazaar. Dave Wilkinson, never renowned for sartorial elegance in his job as senior lecturer at Birmingham Polytechnic, tried some of the more stylish items on himself before reluctantly giving them to the porters who were, with one exception, content with their spoils. But one, a garish vinyl remnant of flower power and obviously a lady's coat, was too much for one porter. His mates thought the same and eventually it was swapped for something more becoming. All this was carried out in a remarkably cheerful and co-operative atmosphere. Fida Hussein, our Sirdar (headman) for the walk-in, had worked with Al before and could take on most of the responsibility himself. It seemed a good beginning and promised, at last, to herald the real start to the expedition. Perhaps now I would be able to unwind, begin work on the film in earnest and turn my thoughts to the mountain ahead.

3

CONCORDIA is the confluence of the Baltoro, Upper Baltoro and Godwin Austen Glaciers, a great T-junction. It was cold, quite incredibly cold, and I was in the depths of self-pity, tired, unacclimatised and disappointed. Only one more day and we would be at K2 Base Camp. Groups of tents were pitched in deep powder snow, hopefully not on top of concealed crevasses. Clusters of porters huddled under tarpaulins or plastic sheets in crude stone sangars, like sheep pens, half filled with powder snow, cooking on the remnants of wood they had brought from lower down, or on primitive paraffin stoves purchased in Rawalpindi. Visibility was down to a few hundred metres, as it had been since we had left Urdokas, two days ago. I had not bothered to try and film since then. My dreams of making the best ever documentary of the Karakoram were already fading. This would have been the stage of the walk-in for all the best views of the great giants: Masherbrum, the Mustagh Tower, Gasherbrum IV and Mitre Peak, culminating in the first, head-on, full frontal view of K2 complete with crashing chords, drum rolls and fanfares of trumpets. In reality the only sign of K2 was the Fullers Logo on the tent opposite. It was also about the limit of visibility. "Who put the 'con' in Concordia?" I asked John Barry bitterly.

Apart from the invisibility problem, I was still feeling under-acclimatised, which seemed grossly unfair because the previous year I had gone to over 5500 metres in Peru with no ill effects, part of it by train and truck. Here we were gaining height far more gradually in the approved medical textbook manner and I was grinding to a halt. Was this what stopping being a thirty-a-day cigarette man as a New Year's resolution had done to me? I had read somewhere that smokers are marginally less prone to pulmonary oedema than non-smokers. If so, it must be the one and only benefit nicotine confers on the human lung. True or false, it all seemed like part of sod's law to me just then.

This general feeling of undeserved

shittiness was not improved by the compulsive way Al had been charging through the villages to reach the mountain. It left little time for all those scenes of light filtering through trees and smoke, of children staring in silent fascination at the hubbub of camp life, and of devout Moslem women scurrying out of sight lest they be defiled by the prying eye of the camera. The thought of having to try to capture this background detail on our return journey was depressing, for it is always psychologically harder to concentrate then.

To cap my special woes, I had picked as my film porter a man called Ghulam who spoke some English and came with a glowing testimonial from Galen Rowell. According to these references there seemed no limit to his abilities as climber and photographer's assistant. But it meant Ghulam had definite ideas about sites for camera positions and I had to expend precious energy convincing him Galen Rowell and I didn't have to film from identical stances.

One spot where I was keen to get in some good footage was at the great rusty red granite spires and towers of the Trango and Cathedral groups. It was ten years since I had accompanied Martin Boysen, Mo Anthoine, Malcolm Howells, Tony Riley and Joe Brown who had made the first ascent of the Nameless Tower, and it was that trip which had made me a climbing cameraman, returning again and again to film, photograph and write about the Karakoram, the Andes, Himalaya and Chinese Pamirs. I was almost childishly keen to see the Nameless Tower once more. Slowly to our left the view opened out and the great shaft appeared. Clouds swirled around it and every so often a vertical arête or patch of snow-sprinkled granite would momentarily appear. Feverishly, for the sky was clouding over by the minute, Ghulam and I toiled to the highest point of the moraines where the view was unimpeded. As I struggled with the tripod the others caught up one by one and plodded past.

"Jim filming his lost youth."

"The Karakoram's answer to the Napes Needle."

"Might solo it on my way back."

Everyone felt obliged to say something

derogatory. I told myself firmly that this meant they were probably secretly rather impressed, and tried not to feel offended, concentrating on framing the Tower through the zoom lens of the Scoopic camera at which point it finally disappeared from view. All 200 porters filed slowly past and Ghulam and I were left sitting on a cold and windy hilltop waiting in the rain. The next stage to Urdokas did not improve and from Urdokas to Concordia we had walked in a near total whiteout.

After our night at Concordia I awoke to a crackling frost-encrusted sleeping bag and a light spray of melting hoar frost detached from the tent roof by the first rays of the sun, finding their way with unerring accuracy onto my exposed nose. From the expressions of four-lettered amazement outside I gathered that there was at last something to see. I was in no hurry to share the view as I was worried that the camera equipment would suffer condensation or simply seize up in the low temperatures, but eventually I unzipped the tent door and ventured out.

Below a pale blue sky I could see down

the Baltoro to the summits of the Paiju peaks, snow-plastered and ethereal. Close at hand Mitre Peak glistened with ice and reflected sunlight under finely sculpted ice flutings and whipped cream cornices. It was hard to believe it only just topped 6000 metres. Behind were the big hills, Gasherbrum IV stately and elegant, the West Face of compelling size and steepness yet with a simplicity of form that was quite breathtaking. Away to the right Chogolisa was from here foreshortened and impressed more through volume than line, as did Broad Peak, whose great bulk and long summit ridge seemed, even from Concordia, to tower above us.

But all these views paled into insignificance when compared with what was now only some twelve miles away at the head of the Godwin Austen Glacier. The sight made my flesh crawl, and took away what little breath I had. K2. There it was, unequivocal, real, present, impassive and quite monumentally huge. A great triangle that hung like a gigantic backdrop to the silent amphitheatre of Concordia. It, too, was draped in snow and in its wintery vastness looked utterly impregnable, yet with a beauty and simplicity of form and balance that gave it a certain lightness that I had not expected from the many photos I had seen taken from this spot.

It was exciting to be able to identify so many of the features that have become household names to climbers. There was the Mushroom, a snowfield ending in a huge sérac on Messner's still unachieved Magic Line. Right of that, splitting the South Face, were the two huge unclimbed ridges. The right-hand was the one tried by Al and Doug in 1983. Above it the Shoulder, apparently a gentle snowslope sweeping up to the Narrows, and the Bottleneck, the gulley leading to the summit snowslopes. It was Luigi Amedeo di Savoia, Duke of Abruzzi, who led the first attempt to climb K2 in 1908. Though he scarcely gained more than the foot of the ridge, the Abruzzi became the route by which the mountain was first ascended in 1954 by Compagnoni and Lacedelli. From Concordia most of the Abruzzi Ridge is in profile and it was easy to pick out the Black Pyramid and the insignificant looking buttress containing House's Chimney. What stories, what legendary names these features evoked—Houston, Wolfe, Gilkey, Bonatti, Puchoz, Lacedelli, Compagnoni, Messner, names that have become indelibly stamped on the history of K2.

As I set up the tripod and gingerly mounted the camera on it, very aware of the real danger of getting frostnipped fingers, which would be embarrassing at such an early stage of the expedition, I was almost relieved that our route, the North-West Ridge, was out of sight behind the left-hand profile of the West Ridge. Carefully I filmed the panorama. After a minute the camera abruptly stopped. With a sinking heart I prayed it had merely frozen, and not seized up. A new battery made no difference and as the spare Scoopic was buried in the depths of a porter load, it became dismally obvious that, with perfect visibility at last, I would now get no more film until after we had reached Base Camp. Sod's law was keeping pace with me.

And yet only hours later as we trudged up the Godwin Austen Glacier I could hardly fail to be uplifted as Broad Peak slid past to my right and K2 appeared bigger and bigger. Soon we could see the chaotic icefall at the bottom of the Savoia Glacier. It was good to know that there was a relatively safe route, hugging the side of Angel Peak, that would avoid this section. And now, only a mile or so ahead, was journey's end. Tucked right into the lowest rocks at the very base of the long spur running south-west from K2 that comprises the Negrotto Col, Angel Peak itself, and Point Negrotto was our Base Camp site. Tiny figures were already scattered around as the porters were chivvied up the last few metres to drop their loads in the right place.

It had been a debatable point where exactly to have Base Camp. The American expedition in 1975, Chris Bonington in 1978, the Poles in 1982 and the successful Japanese West Ridge Expedition in 1981 had all had theirs under the West Face in the middle of the Savoia Glacier. But despite its proximity to the foot of the North-West Ridge, there seemed little real advantage in so desolate a spot. At 5365 metres it was near the point where it is impossible to acclimatise permanently and a slow deterioration sets in. Added to that, the site is in the middle of a snow-covered glacier which becomes increasingly crevasse-ridden as the season goes on, and in fine weather is an almost unbearable sun trap. Our alternative site, just below the 1954 Art Gilkey memorial cairn, was sheltered, and on moraine rather than bare ice. As the winter snow melted it was a place from which it was safe and easy to walk around to the traditional K2 Base Camp area on the long glacial moraine leading towards the foot of the Abruzzi Ridge.

Its only disadvantage was that it seemed threatened by a band of precarious séracs high above but Al reckoned that it was perfectly safe as behind the tent platforms a big hollow, unseen from below, would catch any avalanche which in any case would probably fall down a gully well out of line of the tents. As a Rouse Theory it was only half convincing. This was because of a story Al himself often told with great relish of how in 1983 everyone had fled onto the glacier as a huge mass of ice had roared down the gully. Dusting themselves off from the powder snow that had enveloped them, they cautiously returned to the tents, suddenly conscious that Steve Sustad was missing. Anxiously opening his tent they found him reading with Walkman headphones clamped to his ears, sublimely unaware that the avalanche had occurred! Whether or not this story was found reassuring was up to the individual but I noticed that, on our arrival on 23rd May, Al quickly set his personal tent up as close under the protecting rocks as possible. Phil Burke and Al Burgess also took up residence in what I nicknamed Abruzzi Close, while the rest of us were camped more randomly on the more exposed Chogolisa Crescent. Dave Wilkinson tempted fate by camping a short distance away on the top of a pile of moraine nearest the avalanche gully.

And so we had arrived. From our eyrie we could look across at the main K2 Base Camp site. In the weeks to come a small village of brightly coloured tents would stretch in an untidy line. We called it the Strip after its resemblance to the main street in some mid-western American town. But now there was only the big orange frame tent which must be the Casarottos', and a bit further up a small cluster of tents that would be the French expedition. The Barrards, Michel and Wanda had caught us up and passed us at Paiju campsite while we had taken a rest day. Maurice had seemed even more possessed with urgency to get to the mountain than Al, and had risked a porter strike in pushing ahead so quickly. But he, Liliane and Michel had not got unlimited time on their hands and, although they had temporarily sorted out their finances, they would be facing a huge debt on their return. They had not seemed a homogeneous party. Wanda had been nearly hysterical at the discovery of a large tic burrowing into her hair. She was making a film for Polish TV but didn't seem to be at home with the gear she had been given.

Our Base Camp took some organising but it was imperative to keep the momentum going to Advance Base, which would be in roughly the same place as the earlier expeditions' Base Camps on the Savoia Glacier. Eight porters volunteered for this carry, plus Ghulam who, perhaps disillusioned with me, had managed to inveigle his way into becoming our mail runner. Beyond the first rocky outcrops that skirted the icefall, the plan was that we should travel up and down the glacier between these two camps and on toward Camp 1 on skis with cross-country bindings. The team's skiing ability varied widely from the inevitable athletic stylishness of the Burgess twins and the total competence of former ski instructor, John Barry at one end, to me at the other. Everyone else was in between, though in all honesty there was still a big gap between me and the next worst. For the simple truth was that, apart from one disastrous week in Chamonix several years previously when Al had tried to teach me the rudiments in appalling weather, I had no experience at all, and not a great deal of interest.

Before the trip Al had with his usual unshakable optimism assured me that skiing on the glacier would be no problem at all. "You'll just go in a dead straight line downhill till you get to about eighty miles an hour, when you'll be so scared you'll crash to stop yourself. Then you do it again. That's all there is to it." I knew from past experience that this was unlikely to be the case but, as is often the way before expeditions, one can conveniently blind oneself to reality.

Once we arrived at Base Camp and the eight porters had done their carries, Al divided his climbing spearhead into two groups which inevitably became known as the A team and the B team, and equally inevitably seemed to proceed to try and live up to their labels. The object was to have two small self-contained groups operating more or less independently on the mountain, either pushing fixed ropes out and establishing camps, or in a support role ferrying gear, or resting. In theory there would always be someone out in front and momentum would be maintained. Meanwhile I would operate independently as and when (or "if", I thought privately) I acclimatised, helped by Jim and Bev. The A team was Al, Aid Burgess, Phil Burke and John Porter; the B consisted of John Barry, Dave Wilkinson, Al Burgess and Brian Hall.

Al's decision initially seemed sensible. The twins were by far the strongest climbers and, by separating them for the early stages, he hoped to maximise their potential within each group. Brian and

John Porter were also split up, having climbed a lot together in the past. What Al had not been able to take into account was that, almost from the outset, Brian was in trouble, and it was getting worse. While skiing in Chamonix earlier in the year he had injured his knee. It had stopped him running before the expedition but seemed to be improving slowly. But the 120 miles we had just walked had taken their toll and Brian was in constant pain from what eventually proved to be a very badly torn ligament. This was compounded by persistent headaches and nausea. On his last expedition to Makalu with Doug Scott in 1984, Brian had been knocked unconscious by falling ice and since then he had been plagued by frequent headaches. Now, after only a couple of weeks at Base Camp, it became clear that his problems were not going to go away. He returned on his own from a carry to Camp 1 limping badly, and his face was drawn with strain. Quietly he retreated to his tent where for the next few days, plagued by splitting headaches, he convinced himself at one point that he was suffering from cerebral oedema. He was to take no further part in the expedition, though for some days I hoped he could stay and help with the film, but it was not to be, and Brian sadly decided that home, hospital and an exploratory knee operation were going to be the only sensible options.

Down to three, the B team's chances were not improved by the weather which since our arrival had been more or less bad, with a few brief interludes which could hardly be described as more than fair. On a mountain the size of K2 it is essential to take full advantage of any reasonable weather, and this often means leaving Base Camp in bad weather with only the faintest indication that it might improve. It took one very long day to Camp 1, or two short ones, and then, if conditions allowed, the route could be pushed out on the long mixed face leading onto the ridge itself. But it seemed that the B team were forever doomed to get the worst of it and whatever they did the weather would perversely outwit them. Conversely the A team always seemed to manage to get something done and, as is usual in these situations, couldn't help rubbing the fact in.

Sat in the middle and still contributing little or nothing to the expedition I found these interminable Base Camp wrangles tedious in the extreme. Not that the arguments were often directly about the expedition. They covered a wide range of subjects but almost inevitably it ended up with Jim Hargreaves and John Barry attempting to defend, by volume alone, a cause to which they felt emotionally, if not intellectually, drawn. Unless it involved the opposite sex the twins normally remained quiet, as did Dave Wilkinson, except for the odd perceptive and intelligent comment (by which I mean one I agreed with). And John Porter kept a low profile too. It was Al who invariably provided the opposition, though on subjects like education and law and order I found Jim's views so far to the right of Ghengis Khan it was hard to avoid the temptation to join in. But Al with his mathematician's logic and bewildering (and often wholly imaginary) arrays of facts at his disposal could run rings round all of us if he put his mind to it. Poor John Barry who started arguments for the fun of it was often reduced to an impotent frenzy, as Al led him round in circles. Sometimes it would remain good-humoured but it still became very wearing and certainly not a good way of relaxing on rest days.

It was far more interesting to walk over to the Strip, and as the numbers grew, to make new friendships and renew old ones. When in late June the Strip was at full complement, it was almost impossible to get to the far end. Invitations to so many Base Camp tents on the way took up so much time that the original team earmarked for a visit would be forgotten. There was also a danger of overeating tempting snacks and drinking too many brews. But in the early days the population was not so high and on one early visit Al, Phil and I went to pay our respects to Renato Casarotto, Goretta and the two Basques, Mari and Josema. Al had met them all before and spoke quite good Spanish from his South American forays, though he knew no Italian.

Axes, pitons, karabiners, crampons and clothing were hung neatly round the walls of their big frame tent. In the corner a tiny two-man tent was pitched, giving a weatherproof and draught-free bedroom. Renato Casarotto was not what I had expected. Tall, broad shouldered, and piratically bearded, he seemed in demeanour more like a Northern European, while he explained his plans and philosophy with infectious enthusiasm in affable broken English. Goretta was fair and petite and stayed almost silent, passing round small cups of delicious strong black coffee and homemade cake. She was wearing a large floppy sunhat, enormous fashion sunglasses, check shirt and Helly Hansen fibre pile salopettes. Her classical beauty and grace gave her an illusion of height, though when she and Renato stood side by side he towered over her. It was obvious that they were utterly devoted to each other. The image of the medieval knight in shining armour and the fair lady waiting in the castle came to my mind and stuck there firmly.

Renato told us how upset he had been to find out that other expeditions would also be attempting the route he was trying to climb solo. It put him in a difficult, almost impossible, situation. But he had resolved to keep himself apart and work systematically on his own, fixing rope, self-belaying, descending, jumaring, sack hauling in a labour of love that I found hard to comprehend, but could only admire. Of course he was not new to the Himalayan soloing game and had impeccable qualifications. Ten years of hard soloing in the Alps and Andes, notably the North Face of Huandoy in Peru, and the North-East Pillar of Fitzroy (the Goretta Pillar) in Patagonia led him to the Himalaya where his best route had been the first ascent of the North Peak of Broad Peak in 1983. With Goretta he had also climbed Gasherbrum II in 1985.

He had also been on Messner's 1979 K2 expedition. The two had not hit it off and in his book, *K2, Mountain of Mountains*, Messner loses no time in telling the reader on the very first page that he felt let down by Renato "as a climber". They too had been attempting the South-South-West Ridge, what Messner had dubbed the Magic Line, which runs from the summit to the Negrotto Col and contains some of the mountain's steepest and most technical climbing, both on rock and ice. Messner had backed off it in favour of a conventional (though first oxygen-free) ascent of the Abruzzi. The fact that in 1986 Casarotto had returned to attempt the Magic Line again seemed to indicate a score to be settled. It was interesting that in a profile of Casarotto in *Mountain* magazine in 1984, the Messner expedition is not even mentioned. More recently, in a meeting of "top" high-altitude climbers held in Messner's castle in the Tyrol in October 1985, Messner was told about Casarotto's plans for the Magic Line. "He'll never make it!" was his dismissive comment. If ever a man had a reason to succeed, it was Renato Casarotto.

Impressed with Renato's intensity and almost touchingly innocent view of mountains and climbs (he had seemed quite genuinely distressed when Al explained that we would be using fixed ropes on our route, perhaps seeing it as something beneath Al's dignity to attempt), we sauntered over to the next tents where Al, switching languages, took over in fluent French.

"I wonder how good Al's Korean is?" I muttered to Phil, for we had been told that a vast army of Korean climbers was about to arrive.

For reasons that were never entirely clear to me, Wanda and Michel had fallen out and, although still climbing with Maurice and Liliane, were not really together. Wanda had borrowed one of our small summit tents to avoid sharing with Michel on the route. It seemed a terrible waste of effort and increase in weight, but ours was not to reason why. They were all getting frustrated at the mediocre weather, though I was surprised that at this early stage Maurice was already thinking about a summit bid.

Our own progress was still sketchy. Camp 1 had been established at 6000 metres in the cwm below the mixed face leading to the ridge at 6800 metres. But progress on the face was painfully slow. Constant snowfalls meant that on occasions it was all anyone could do to reach the bottom of the fixed ropes. Sometimes by the time the high point had been reached, so much energy had been expended clearing the ropes and breaking trail that no new ground could be gained. It was already becoming a battle that was slowly to grind everyone down.

As for myself, the first weeks at Base Camp were terribly demoralising. It took several attempts before I could even progress beyond the rocky buttresses and onto the Savoia Glacier itself, and then two attempts to reach Advance Base. Skinning uphill I found initially desperate and doing so with any sort of load was purgatorial. But my total lack of skill made itself felt on the descents where I fell over constantly. I was in tears of despair, frustration and exhaustion on one occasion. Every novice skier experiences something similar but at around 6000 metres, in a near white-out, on my own, and carrying a rucksack, I wondered just how much more stupid I could get before men in white coats would lead me away. Or, more realistically, before I fell down a crevasse and was killed, for my inability to maintain any sort of control was potentially dangerous. Yet without skis the chances of a crevasse fall were even higher.

The real problem was that though Jim and Bev were far more confident skiers than I, they lacked big mountain experience, so were not prepared to go above Base Camp, apart from on a very occasional carry. They were understandably daunted by the traverse of the buttresses which, while little more than easy scrambling, were still quite serious. Short sections of fixed rope helped, but there was always a threat of avalanches from the séracs high on Angel Peak, and they never managed to get above Advance Base. I sighed for the support I had had from David Wilson on Mount Kongur. A political adviser to Hong Kong (and since its Governor), David was a keen hill walker and fell runner. We ended up an improbable pair climbing onto the South Ridge of Kongur and had spent a couple of nights camped on the summit of a small snow dome on its lower reaches in order to film the climbers as they ascended the ridge. But from an early stage it was all too clear that Bev and Jim did not see themselves in this role and I was forced to operate solo.

The first time I actually made it to Advance Base I had skinned painfully slowly up the first long rise on the glacier. The early morning chill gave way to oven heat as the sun beat down into the airless valley, my progress slowed and I rested frequently. The second uphill section was interminable and, head down, leaning on my ski sticks, I forced myself onwards, not bothering to look up. Suddenly I became aware of my surroundings. "Bugger me!" The words escaped my lips though there was no-one to hear them (or thankfully carry out my command!). The vast West Face of K2 was in view before me like several Eiger North Faces piled on top of each other. It was even more dramatic than the view at Concordia. Three thousand vertical metres separated me from the summit across which plumes of snow were being blown into an inky blue sky.

My eyes were drawn to the fateful snow-field below the crest of the West Ridge where Nick Estcourt had been avalanched. He had written me a wish-you-were-here postcard a few days before his death. Now, eight years later, I was. Advance Base was only a hundred metres further and I sat down for a last rest, thinking about Nick with a light heart and with a clear vision of him that somehow had been suppressed in all those years before. As I approached the tents I could see four tiny dots far ahead of me as the A team moved up to the slopes below Camp 1—not for me this time, but feeling far better than I had done for weeks, I spent the night on my own before returning once more to Base Camp.

It was around this time that the inevitable occurred. At 11.30 p.m. one night, as everyone lay nodding off, there was a crash as a vast sérac fell from Angel Peak. Thousands of tons of ice erupted into the gully behind Base Camp, accompanied by a cloud of pulverised ice dust and a gale force wind. I awoke to find the tent fabric pressed against my face. Momentarily confused and frightened, I couldn't decide if the tent itself was moving or being crushed. Jim Hargreaves had made a double quick exit from his tent, sprinting sockless and scantily clad to the rocks behind Al and Phil. He was enveloped in ice dust and, danger over, picked his way agonisingly back over the sharp snow-covered scree. From the warmth of my sleeping bag I heard shouts of inquiry and reassurance, one coming from as far away as Casarotto whose Liaison Officer had seen the avalanche. So, too, had Steve

Boyer, a doctor with the American South-South-West Ridge Expedition, that had only just arrived on the Strip. Standing outside his tent to relieve himself he saw, eerily lit by the light of the moon, the huge cloud envelope our Base Camp. His comment had been elegant in its simplicity.

"Holy shit! . . . 'Bye 'bye Brits!"

4

BY the beginning of June new faces were arriving on the Strip almost every day and processions of porters up from Concordia were beginning to resemble scenes from some Hollywood epic where slaves toil across a gigantic screen to build the pyramids. The Americans, from Portland, Oregon, who were going for the South-South-West Ridge lost no time in visiting us. There were eight climbers, plus Chelsea Monike, their Base Camp Manager. Of course she had to put up with outrageous flirting from most of us, plus the obligatory ribbing about her name, which must have mystified her, as Chelsea is an uncommon but not unknown girl's name in the States.

"I suppose it could have been worse, Aston Villa Monike or Rotherham United Monike . . ."

But Chelsea soon gave as good as she got and the whole team seemed a warm and cohesive unit. On paper they appeared to lack experience, and for many of them it was their first Himalayan venture. We wondered if it wasn't a rather over-ambitious objective but were impressed at the quiet systematic way in which they approached the undertaking. What they thought of us as they sat, somewhat bemused, in our tent while we all tried to tell the most outrageous stories to a new audience, was anyone's guess.

During one spell of bad weather I was at Base Camp with Bev and Jim when two familiar-looking figures slowly climbed the last scree-covered slopes to the tents. As they approached I recognised Kurt Diemburger and Julie Tullis. I had heard rumours that they were accompanying the big Italian Quota 8000 expedition which had arrived a few days before without them, and I assumed I had got the story wrong. I greeted Kurt and Julie with slightly mixed feelings. I had known them both on and off since 1982, when, out of the blue, they had arrived in Bristol and spent several days in the Media Department at college editing some of the film they had shot that summer on Nanga Parbat. Our paths had then crossed again at the Kendal Film Festival in 1983 when once more they had arrived unexpectedly. Julie had persuaded us to let Kurt show a film at the last minute and subsequently asked us £200 for the privilege, which we could ill afford.

I occasionally saw Julie at Trade Fairs and climbing do's and yet could never quite decide what to think of her. On one hand she was a bright, attractive and apparently conventional housewife and mother from Tunbridge Wells who looked much younger than her forty-seven years. On the other she was a rather bossy "head girl" who, through her devotion, almost amounting to hero-worship, of Kurt, had come to see herself as a world-class mountaineer in her own right. For despite her ascent with Kurt in 1984 of Broad Peak, and two previous attempts on both K2 and Nanga Parbat, her actual mountaineering experience was rather limited and certainly had not got the foundation of Scottish winter and extreme alpine climbing that most, if not all, British hard climbers take as a matter of course.

But she was strong, fit and very determined, qualities that are as important as any in Himalayan climbing. She was also a very competent rock climber, through her many years instructing on the sandstone outcrops of Harrison's Rocks and High Rocks where she and her husband Terry had made their lives. I had started my own climbing in the late 'fifties at Harrison's and had dim memories of Julie and Terry in the Sandstone Club. They became a bit clearer when I remembered that they ran the celebrated "Festerhaunt", a climbers' café in the village of Groombridge, near Harrison's.

Her late arrival on the international mountaineering scene had come out of the blue, through her friendship and film partnership with Kurt Diemburger. Since then she had changed a lot and I was very aware that she was fiercely competitive as a climber, a film-maker and an independent woman. I was always conscious that my reaction to Julie could be accused of being flavoured with sour grapes. I was never quite sure if she thought of me as a rival, or indeed if I felt that about her.

Kurt Diemburger is a living legend. At fifty-four, medium height, heavily built and, like me, prone to put on weight easily, he radiated a massive self-confidence, amounting at times to self-importance. Since his first ascent of Broad Peak with Buhl, Schmuck and Wintersteller in 1957, and subsequent epic on Chogolisa when Hermann Buhl stepped through a cornice on the summit ridge and fell to his death. Diemburger has been one of the very great mountaineers of the century. He remains the only person to have made the first ascent of two 8000 metre peaks (Broad Peak and Dhaulagiri) and he has also climbed Everest, Gasherbrum II, Makalu, and Tirich Mir, and made many expeditions to every major mountain range in the world.

A confirmed romantic and a talented writer (his autobiography, *Summits and Secrets*, is a classic of mountaineering literature), his interests had turned to film in later years and in Julie he found the perfect partner, as sound recordist and assistant cameraman. Previously I had found him Kurt by name and curt by nature, but now sitting outside the Base Camp tents in watery sunshine, he was relaxed and affable. With a proud gleam in his eye, he confessed that it was exactly twenty-nine years to the day that he and Hermann Buhl had climbed Broad Peak. It was a curiously moving statement and I was suddenly conscious that here was a major part of Himalayan climbing history in the flesh. He looked down to Concordia and beyond to the graceful floating trapezium of Chogolisa. It was not difficult to guess his thoughts.

Over tea and biscuits he and Julie told us that they were indeed with the Italians but because there was another cameraman with the team they were not expected to film much lower down.

"It's a real holiday for us, we can just do what we want," Julie explained, although I was never entirely clear what their exact roles were. They always operated as a self-contained twosome and their films frequently seemed to be about each other. They were acclimatising slowly and went for frequent excursions around Base Camp, on one occasion going as far as Windy Gap at the head of the Godwin Austen Glacier to get magnificent views back at the North-East Face of K2. They were also planning a trip around to the Savoia Glacier and up to the Saddle from where they could look down into China and the approach to K2 from the north, where they had been in 1983. On that occasion, again filming with an Italian team, they had both reached 8000 metres on the North Ridge of K2 before being stopped by a storm at their top camp.

They were diffident about their plans for this year, but I didn't doubt for one minute that, given half a chance, they would be going for the summit, though I always found their priorities somewhat confusing. It seems to me that in order to make a successful film one's own climbing ambition must take second place and on a mountain like K2, attempting both could be over-ambitious. I wondered whether Kurt and Julie in their heart of hearts had ever actually resolved the dilemma. But now, as the evening light played on the triple summits of Broad Peak high above us, they both seemed happy simply to be here. Seeing them in the environment they both loved so much helped me sympathise with them and I resolved to try to forget my sometimes uncharitable feelings. As they left Julie told me that she, too, had hardly ever skied before and that, like us, they were using skins on the glacier. We had found something in common and laughed at our obviously identically inept performances.

The comings and goings that made life at Base Camp a much more entertaining place than if we had been alone still couldn't disguise the fact that our own progress on the North-West Ridge was giving some cause for concern. The long mixed slope up to the crest of the ridge seemed never-ending. We had managed to keep radio contact via a "rebro" unit loaned by Plessey, an elaborate receiver and transmitter powered by a solar panel, set up in the middle of the Savoia Glacier. This bounced signals around the dog-leg of the glacier and we could speak to Advance Base, Camp 1 and, when it was eventually established, Camp 2. But calls at seven each evening were often of disappointing progress or none at all. The perennial problem was the weather. Climbing in marginal conditions and making little or no progress is demoralising but also poses a logistical conundrum to which there is no satisfactory answer. The first principle of sieging a long complex route is that continuous progress must be maintained. Sitting out bad weather means all the food and fuel that have taken so much time and effort to carry are used up with nothing to show for it. Yet to go down to Base Camp means more hard work will be needed to regain the height lost, establish tracks and dig out buried fixed ropes.

Inevitably frustration grew and the B team was having to bear the brunt of it, being accused of not pulling their weight, not carrying enough, and returning to Base Camp too easily. Brian was by now out of action and waiting for the return of Ghulam from his first mail run before he left for home; Dave Wilkinson, who was the slowest of the seven climbers, always did his share of carrying but because he was so slow could never do much lead climbing; John Barry, who was rather faster, still found keeping up with Al Burgess so hard that Al inevitably ended up doing most of the leading. The B team were getting upset by the niggling and it seemed high time to form a different plan of attack.

Al Rouse was determined to lead from

the front and was pushing himself, as always, very hard, having little energy left for organisational matters. He had, as he had done on both Everest in winter and on Kongur, developed a desperate throat infection that reduced him to a husky whisper, not the best way of dominating a vociferous group like ourselves.

When Brian left I felt very near to going with him for the filming was going badly. Camera and sound gear were continually breaking down. Brian, in fact, had been the most practical person and was able to improvise repairs. I still found my own climbing performance disappointing, but during the next fine weather spell I wended my way back to Advance Base with the intention of getting to Camp 1 and perhaps beyond. At last the final rope-lengths onto the ridge had been completed and Camp 2 was being established. Suddenly, everyone seemed hopeful that progress would be quicker and that, if the ropes could be run out from 6800 to around 8000 metres and another camp put in, we would be ready for a summit attempt. There did seem to be a tendency to say this as fast as possible and hope that by doing so the difficulties would be minimised, for I couldn't help thinking that the next 1000 metres would almost certainly be what would sort us out. But suddenly with the weather perking up and feeling far better myself I joined in the general air of optimism.

Three days later I stood gasping in the cold air but hot sunshine at the foot of the first fixed rope leading up round a small rock buttress guarding the hanging valley at the entrance of which I knew Camp 1 was pitched. From the vast expanse of the Savoia Glacier I had just skied up in the early morning, I could see no sign of either the camp or anyone else. At the foot of the ropes was a sack of film equipment I had carried up the day before. On my back was my personal gear. I was in a quandary, for taking one without the other made little sense and I doubted whether I could possibly climb the remaining 300 metres to Camp 1, descend and reascend in the same day. Pondering my best course of action, I was startled and relieved to hear my name shouted. High above a minute figure, which I eventually recognised as Phil

Burke, was abseiling down to give me a hand with the other sack.

Delighted that the problem was solved I painfully ground up the ropes until about two rope-lengths from the top, when Al also appeared and relieved me of my sack. After a strange little diversion across the false floor of a crevasse threatened by a sérac, a few feet of steep ice lead out into a narrow valley and, at the last moment, the sight of the tents. Great. I hadn't really expected to get there until the next day and was so pleased that I had an attack of verbal diarrhoea that lasted most of the afternoon, while John Porter and John Barry made brews and listened to my incoherent ramblings. They were both pleased to see me "off the ground at last" so to speak, and I was duly flattered.

John Porter and Al were going up to Camp 2 early next morning and Phil and Aid Burgess were having a rest day. John Barry and Dave and Al Burgess were bound for a real rest at Base Camp. Phil and Aid volunteered to spend the following afternoon, 21st June, filming on the fixed ropes below Camp 1. It was a magnificent day with not a cloud in the sky. From the camp a fantastic panorama stretched away, dominated at close range by the Savoia peaks, with a glimpse beyond of the Mustagh Tower, as well as other unknown spires and domes. Behind the camp was the colossal North-West Buttress of K2, a monster bulging pear shape of featureless rock seamed with ice. On the right was the crest of the West Ridge with the summit of Angel Peak sweeping gracefully beyond it. Now, although it was still above us, we could look across instead of craning our necks. That, however, was what we still had to do to see the summit rocks of K2 itself.

In the clear air the summit looked quite near, until the rest of the route was mentally accommodated. Then, with sinking heart, it became all too obvious that Camp 1 was still almost at the bottom of the mountain. Above us, some half mile up the narrow valley, was the start of the fixed ropes leading up around and over small buttresses in a very prominent arête. From there a traverse right across a wide gully led to the foot of another buttress and gully leading eventually to the crest of the ridge. It was in itself a respectable alpine route, comparable with, say, the North Face of the Courtes, yet was only a small feature in the gargantuan surroundings. Above, the ridge seemed broad and easy-angled for a few hundred metres, until abruptly butting up against the massive rocky sweep of the Upper Ridge. From photographs I had always imagined this to be a sharp pinnacled ridge whose crest would have to be more or less followed in its entirety. Even from Camp 1 it was possible to see that this was not the case and that there was no "skyline" as such, just a rounded broken mass of buttresses with no clear definition. The Poles in 1982 had ventured well into China by following a rising gully leading leftwards towards the North Ridge. Would we have to do the same?

Al had previously enthused wildly about the thrill of doing really hard technical free climbing at 7500 metres and evolved an absurd theory that, move for move, it would be no different to sea level. Even he must have realised it was patent nonsense for he didn't pursue the argument for long and acknowledged, with the inevitable shamefaced grin, my extension of his theory. This was that if hard climbing was no harder than sea level then easy climbing must be even easier, and walking up the last few feet to the top would be so easy that there was no real point in doing it at all, therefore we may as well go home now, claiming success before it became a walkover.

On the same subject Al, who could persuade himself of the truth of almost anything he wanted to believe, said he thought all the climbing on K2 couldn't really be described as such because it was all walking or scrambling at the most. "Scrambling" was a favourite epithet used by Al to describe any form of climbing within his limitations. Thus the middle section of London Wall, a vicious gritstone route in Derbyshire that in the mid-seventies was reckoned to be one of the hardest rock climbs in Britain, was in 1986 "mere scrambling" on the Al Rouse Bullshit Scale. John Barry once observed that anything Al said had to be either divided or multiplied by at least four, the trick was knowing which one to do.

For Al, who was climbing with John Porter, the decision to follow the Polish route seemed the most logical and while I filmed Phil and Aid in a startlingly beautiful afternoon light, high above John and Al were at last making real progress.

John Porter was very much the dark horse of the expedition. A climber who does not seek the public eye but who, over the years, has amassed an impressive number of expeditions, including several joint Anglo-Polish ventures, one of the strangest being to the Wakan Corridor in Afghanistan. They travelled through Russia and back as Russian troops prepared to invade. What's more, neither John nor the Poles had permits. John explained that in Iron Curtain countries there are three ways to travel—with the proper papers which are impossible to obtain, with useless papers which land you in more trouble than they are worth, or with no papers at all. This he had found works best of all! John had also climbed a new route on Changabang in the Garhwal Himalaya, and had been with Alex MacIntyre when he was killed attempting a new route on the South Face of Annapurna. I had known John since the first Kendal Film Festival in 1979. He lives in

Millom in the bottom left-hand corner of the Lake District. Because of his remoteness and also because of his aforementioned dreamy and intellectual nature he often seemed slightly withdrawn and otherworldly. Al rated him very highly indeed and, although in Britain they didn't climb a lot together, they had done so on Everest and now were performing well again on the ridge.

It was exciting to feel the good vibes of progress emanating from above and I was preparing to push myself up the ropes with the ultimate ambition of reaching the ridge, Camp 2 and possibly, as Al had always hoped, my "magic" target of 7000 metres. I was not confident that I would achieve this on my first attempt but was keen at least to ferry some film gear as far up the ropes as possible. Resting in camp often produces a feeling of euphoria and it is all too easy to forget simple tasks. Packing a basic film kit of camera, lenses, filmstock and accessories was a job just about within my intellectual capabilities. As late afternoon turned to evening the light became more and more intense. The summit rocks had an unearthly glow below the black vault of night sky. Not a breath of wind stirred. I couldn't miss it and hastily unpacked the cameras again. The shadow of K2 above was vast and oppressive, the view away from it sublime.

At seven the radio crackled into life from above as Al radioed down the day's progress to Aid. Then Base Camp came in and Al Burgess and Aid exchanged news. Phil and I listened for any interesting information, which seemed to be unforthcoming, and sensing the call was about to end I started back to the warmth of the tent and my sleeping bag, for by now the sun had gone and it was bitterly cold. Then Al Burgess's voice came on once more—strangely hesitant and strained.

"Just one more thing, kid. Be careful of avalanches on the face." A pause, then, "Two of the Americans were killed this morning."

The words, like hammer blows, seemed in their simple finality to hang in the air for one long moment.

"Oh, shit." Then, "What happened?"

"A huge avalanche from the Negrotto Col—didn't stand a chance."

Another pause: "Tell them from us

we're all very sorry." Aid signed off and returned to the tent he was sharing with Phil.

There was not much to say and I closed the door of my own tent and tried to come to terms with the news. For in an awful way it was not totally unexpected. With so many climbers on K2 it was statistically almost inevitable that there would be an accident. Though we had never discussed it openly, perhaps fearing that to do so would be tempting fate, it was something that seemed to be lurking under the surface. Now on a beautiful calm day, which Aid, Phil and I had spent messing around filming, story telling and relaxing, two lifeless bodies who, this time yesterday would have been preparing, like me, for an early start, were lying somewhere on K2, their lives over and done. Who were they, I wondered. The day before I left for Advance Base I had talked at length to two lanky Americans who had dropped in for a brew. One was an architect whose laid-back conversation was amusing and interesting. I hoped he wasn't one of them.

Suddenly everything looked different. These two deaths had jolted me out of my assumption that I was cast in a virtually risk-free role on the expedition, following a route kindly made safe for me by the lead climbers. But suppose the fine weather had caused a gradual destabilising of the slope? Perhaps the whole lot was due for a major collapse? I was spending more time on my own on the Savoia Glacier than the others and, if and when I got onto the fixed ropes to Camp 2, I would be exposing myself to stonefall and avalanche danger for longer than the other swifter climbers. Ignorance had been bliss. Now every sense was on edge.

Unable to sleep, uncomfortable despite lying on double Karrimats and in a luxurious Everest sleeping bag, I tossed and turned fretfully, my thoughts returning again and again to the Americans. How must the rest of their team be feeling?

At around midnight I heard, to my surprise, a brief pattering of snow on the tent and a gentle flapping of the fabric in a breeze which had sprung up—very strange as only a few hours earlier the sky had been absolutely clear. I lay awake staring into the darkness. The last thing I wanted to do was set out for Camp 2. I waited for three a.m. and the dreaded moment when I would have to start brewing and getting ready. But first I unzipped the tent and peered outside. Swathes of mist were hanging over the Savoia Glacier, and a sinister halo enveloped the moon. It looked frightening and ominous. Was the weather about to break yet again? I was torn with indecision. Then the noise of Aid's tent being undone and a reassuring flat Holmfirth accent stated: "I wouldn't be going up those ropes if I were you, youth, not with it looking like this." Thank you, Aid, I thought, from the bottom of my heart. With relief I lay back for a few more hours' sleep.

It was another fine day, but tell-tale signs of a weather change were in the air. A slight haze was forming either of moisture in the atmosphere or dust blown over from China. Whatever it was, it seemed unlikely that the fine weather would last much longer. It now seemed a good idea to go down, for I had spent five nights above Base Camp and in any case I couldn't justify spending any more time eating the food in Camp 1 with nothing to show for it.

Below the fixed ropes I picked up the dreaded skis again. I had devised a marginally better way of getting downhill. This was simply to keep the skins on, which slowed me down considerably, but it was still fun to glide effortlessly back to Advance Base. Below that I got increasingly neurotic as I lurched, only half in control, across crevasses and into slushy puddles that mercifully were not as deep as I knew they could be. I found falling over with a rucksack on terribly wearing and at a height of 5500 metres it took minutes to recover, panting uncontrollably before heaving myself up again. But at last it was over and only the last half mile of scrambling around the buttresses above Base Camp remained. Shattered and suddenly running out of energy, I slithered down and across the last section of fixed ropes. Three weeks earlier they had seemed desperate to negotiate. Now they were barely necessary. For once the welcome sight of Base Camp was tempered by sobering thoughts of what I would hear when I reached there. Al Burgess had told us on the morning radio call that a body had been recovered from the avalanche.

It was, as I had feared, the body of Alan Pennington, the architect with whom I had chatted a few days earlier. With expedition leader, John Smolich, he had been at the American Camp 1 in the snow basin below the wide couloir leading to the Negrotto Col. They had only just left the tents when at 5.30 a.m. a huge boulder just above Camp 2 was dislodged by the first rays of the sun. It had previously been assumed so safe that fixed ropes were attached to it. It had fallen into the couloir triggering a massive slab avalanche that had broken off like an inverted staircase, sending thousands upon thousands of tons of snow and ice into the basin; the huge scar it left was visible from Concordia. John and Alan were engulfed. Team mates Brian Hukari and Steve Boyer found Alan's body later the same day. He had tried to run for it and was only yards from the edge of the debris. There was no sign of John. Alan's body had been carried down to Base Camp and buried at the Gilkey memorial. I was selfishly relieved to have missed the impromptu service attended by all those at

Base Camp, but John Barry, who on his own admission had not normally got much time for funerals, described this one as the most moving he had attended. Afterwards some of the American team came down for brews in our Base Camp tent and talked quietly about John and Alan. Apparently Alan on a previous visit to the Gilkey memorial had taken a photo, at arm's length, of the view down a cleft in the rocks, but for some reason drew back from looking down himself into what was shortly to become his own tomb.

5

THE next day, 23rd June, we were all confined to Base Camp in threatening weather. John Porter and Al Rouse had made good progress, running out eleven rope-lengths up the ramp line of the ridge and reaching a high point of 7400 metres. John, by now acclimatised and in fine form, had suggested during their last push that they took off for what would have been a very bold, alpine-style summit bid. Al, who was still suffering from his throat problems, had demurred. In retrospect John wondered if they would have stood a chance or whether it was merely a bout of high-altitude optimism.

Thoughts of Alan Pennington and John Smolich were never far away—had they made an avoidable mistake or were they just plain unlucky? The Americans had appeared to be doing everything right and it seemed somehow unfair that they had been so cruelly singled out. Talking to Chelsea, who had been very close to both

Alan and John, she voiced a feeling that was shared by all of us.

"I know it sounds silly, but I just wish that they had been here longer and got higher on the mountain—they've even been deprived of that satisfaction."

The Americans had decided to abandon their expedition—a desperately difficult decision to make and one where whatever is decided will be unlikely to be accepted with equanimity by everyone. It is often assumed that any fatality should almost automatically mean the expedition being abandoned, but there are many precedents for carrying on. In areas where access is difficult and costs are high, there is what may seem to some to be a sordidly materialistic motivation for continuing. People's reactions are surprisingly varied. On K2 in 1978 the team was split after the death of Nick Estcourt: Peter Boardman and Chris Bonington wanting to go on, while Joe Tasker and Doug Scott didn't. The decision to carry on is invariably accompanied by the justification that "it is what he would have wanted" and the decision to abandon is mainly out of consideration for next of kin. I must admit to finding both justifications slightly dubious. I am never very sure what any of my deceased friends would have wanted, beyond, I imagine, a very strong desire to stay alive. We never openly discussed what we would have done in similar circumstances, but I have no doubt that after two deaths we would have come to the same decision as the Americans.

The accident had one immediate repercussion. The Italian expedition, Quota 8000, that had also been on the South-South-West Ridge, decided to abandon their route forthwith and change to the Abruzzi. They maintained that in any case they had separate permission for each route from the Ministry of Tourism and though this was later confirmed, at the time there were some doubts expressed about the validity of their claim. It was easy to sympathise with their decision, for the approach to the Negrotto Col, even before the avalanche, seemed highly dangerous.

These events must have seemed an inauspicious welcome to the Polish expedition under the leadership of Janusz Majer, which had arrived on the day before the accident, 20th June. They had intended to reach the Negrotto Col via the Savoia Glacier and establish their Base Camp near the site of our Advanced Base. Their porters had refused to carry on to the glacier and our Liaison Officer Agha had irritated Janusz by refusing to help or encourage them. So they had been forced to camp on the Strip, and start the ridge by the "normal" way.

The Poles were not alone. The threatened South Korean mega-expedition, which we had been told consisted of forty climbers and 500 porters, was also arriving in a succession of small parties. (Their true numbers proved to be a mere nineteen climbers and 290 porters.) The day before the Poles arrived, a seven-man Austrian expedition bound for the Abruzzi Ridge, led by Alfred Imitzer, turned up on the Strip and promptly roped off their Base Camp site, thus deterring visitors. Last but by no means least was the Herrligkoffer Karakoram Expedition 1986. This was a semi-commercial undertaking led by the legendary Dr. Karl Herrligkoffer, most of whose sixteen members had paid 12,000 Deutschmarks to join. They were camped at the far end of the Strip and because of this it took some time before anyone managed to walk the extra 400 metres to visit them: previous attempts, as mentioned before, being thwarted by excessive hospitality offered en route.

When John Barry and I finally got there it was not the doctor we met but an equally celebrated name. I immediately recognised the dashing, almost film-star, good looks of Norman Dyhrenfurth, who despite his sixty-eight years is still as active and enthusiastic as many men in their forties. I was impressed at his encyclopaedic knowledge of mountaineering and his fund of stories of people I knew both from expeditions and film projects. He was here to film for West German TV.

As seems all too common with Herrligkoffer's expeditions, this one was already fraught with ill-will and controversy. We had heard rumours and I was curious as to what had happened, assuming that by the time we had heard the stories they had been exaggerated beyond recognition. But as Dyhrenfurth explained the events of the previous weeks I could only shake my head in bewilderment.

When the expedition (Dr. Herrligkoffer's twenty-second) reached Paiju campsite he realised he hadn't enough cash to pay the porters. Credit cards being unheard of in Baltistan, he was forced to return to Skardu by helicopter to try and cash traveller's cheques (an equally unlikely proposition). It was an incredible piece of mismanagement, for whatever reasons.

By the time he had caught up with the expedition, which had permission for both Broad Peak and K2, and had been helicoptered in to Broad Peak Base Camp with his companion, Doris Kustermann, the expedition had already split into those trying K2 and those for Broad Peak and both teams had changed their original plans. On Broad Peak Peter Wörgötter, their climbing leader, had reverted to the original route, rather than attempting a route first tried by a Herrligkoffer expedition as long ago as 1954.

On K2 the situation was more complex. Herrligkoffer had permission for the Doug Scott Spur, the route tried in 1983 that emerges onto the Shoulder. (This explains presumably why we were not on the rib ourselves, but on the North-West Ridge.) The two strongest climbers on the expedition, Jerzy Kukuczka and Tadeusz Piotrowski, both from Poland, had designs on another spur well to the left that would lead almost directly to the summit, emerging onto the Abruzzi Ridge about 300 metres from the top. This was a line briefly explored and rejected by Reinhold Messner in 1979. It was threatened by séracs in its central section and in the event of bad weather could be a death trap. Three Swiss members supporting the Poles thought the line unjustifiably dangerous and wanted to transfer to the Abruzzi, but were told either to toe the line or consider themselves excluded from the expedition. Herrligkoffer, who had celebrated his seventieth birthday in bed at the foot of Broad Peak, had dragged himself up to K2 Base Camp to issue this ultimatum. Dyhrenfurth had supported the Swiss, pointing out that the Poles weren't even on the route that permission had been given for. But to no avail.

To say that Dyhrenfurth was disillusioned with Herrligkoffer would be to understate the case. He reminisced fondly about Don Whillans' apt nickname "Sterlingscoffer" and regaled us with stories of his notorious International Everest Expedition in 1971: some were familiar, some new. Dyhrenfurth obviously had tremendous respect for Don Whillans and no little affection as well. Don had died suddenly of a heart attack in the summer of 1985. Away in Peru I didn't get the news until my arrival at Heathrow. Over the last few years I had (rather to my surprise) become very friendly with Don and done a fair amount of easy rock climbing with him in Cornwall, Derbyshire and Wales. The shock of his death and sense of loss felt by so many people was a measure of his stature as a man and a mountaineer. Talking about him with Norman Dyhrenfurth in the shadow of K2, the mountain he had wanted to climb on his last expedition, reminded me of some of his classic one-liners, many of them pointedly appropriate, in particular his memorable assessment of a climber who shall remain nameless: "'E knows 'e's a world-class climber, you think 'e is, I'm not so sure, but 'as anyone bothered to tell the mountain?"

Later Dyhrenfurth showed me an ancient cine-camera. "Look at this, it's the same camera I used on Lhotse in 1955 and it's still going strong. Amazing, isn't it?"

I said that it was even more amazing that its owner was, a thought that appealed to Dyhrenfurth and we left in good humour, returning to our Base Camp via what had become known as La Manche, a fast-flowing glacial stream cutting off the Strip from our site.

It was accident, not design, that had isolated the British team from the rest of Europe (and indeed the world) but I felt a strong rapport developing between most, if not all, of the expeditions at Base Camp. At times the drab surroundings took on the appearance of a medieval jousting match, as gaily coloured tents and flags flapped in the wind. For the Strip was almost always windy and visitors to our camp were struck by its sheltered calm, making it possible to sunbathe on folding chairs outside the tents. Visits each way were frequent and what I imagine to be a sort of Olympic village atmosphere prevailed. This was a combination of friendship, wary respect and, deep down, undertones of rivalry, but not overt or bitter. As Al once said the numbers of people who regularly go to the world's highest and hardest mountains are not that great and everyone was aware of everyone else's track record. Like the travelling circuses of top golfers or tennis pros who have to live with each other, there was no room for major argument, and on K2 there was no need. A variety of objectives was being attempted in a variety of ways by a rich and varied group of people. I felt, and I know Norman Dyhrenfurth, Michel Parmentier and others did, too, that it was a rare privilege to be part of such an illustrious company.

The deaths of Alan and John had temporarily overshadowed everything else, but while we were above Camp 1 we had also received vague radio messages from Base Camp that on the Abruzzi Ridge, Maurice and Liliane, Michel and Wanda were within striking distance of the summit. One of the last two or three days must, we assumed, have been their summit day, but there was no firm confirmation of this. The Basque pair, Mari Abrego and Josema Casimiro, were also high on the Abruzzi (they had joined in with Renato Casarotto for mutual convenience but had in practice climbed independently). On the afternoon of the 25th Al had been across to the Strip socialising. He returned to Base Camp, a slightly incongruous figure clad in yellow, green and red striped rock climbing tights and carrying a large red and white golfing umbrella.

"Um . . . more bad news I'm afraid. Maurice and Liliane are missing."

The news received from Italian radio contact at Base Camp was vague but ominous. The weather by now was bad and high on the Shoulder huge snow plumes were billowing away into the storm-shrouded sky. Swirling lenticular clouds like flying saucers settled over Broad Peak. There was no firm news of Michel or Wanda. We all knew what "missing" really meant but until we had final confirmation it seemed best to try and pretend that there would be a happy ending, however unlikely this might be.

The next day most of us wandered over to the Strip, gathering in the Italian tent. Like ours it was an elaborate North Face Dome tent capable of seating about fifteen people. Unlike ours it had solar-powered electric lights, a flat floor and was remarkably clean. It was one of three such tents surrounded by a small village of personal tents. It was like stepping into a civilised and wealthy country house from a slum. I was impressed.

The Italians had their radio open ready to receive messages. Over cups of coffee we began to piece together what was going on. Apparently Maurice, Liliane, Michel and Wanda had all reached the summit on the 23rd and had bivouacked at 8300 metres on the descent. The Basques, Mari and Josema, also got to the top and descended to around 8000 metres. The following morning Michel had descended first in an attempt to catch up with the Basques in the hope of borrowing some gas (vital to maintain fluid intake), for they had run out. Wanda had followed and caught up with Michel but Maurice and Liliane were lagging behind. Mari and Josema had also run out of gas and they descended to the French Camp 3 at 7800 metres. Michel had waited for Maurice and Liliane to catch them up but to no avail. Wanda and the Basques had continued down.

Meanwhile members of the Italian expedition on their own attempt had met Michel but in the face of deteriorating weather decided to turn back. Benoît Chamoux, a young French climber with the Italian expedition, tried to persuade Michel to come down. Michel was adamant that he could not abandon Maurice and Liliane without making some attempt to find them. Benoît had left Michel with a radio and descended rapidly. Now in Base Camp he was pacing the tent anxiously, as the full implications of what had happened gradually dawned on us. For now Michel, high on the Shoulder, was attempting to descend in a white-out and gale-force winds down a featureless snow slope, knowing that somewhere below him was a sérac barrier and, at a gap in the séracs, the beginning of the fixed ropes and the path to safety.

As we sat there listening to the fragments of the story and tried to make sense of them, I remembered a harrowing account in Joe Tasker's book *Savage Arena*. In 1980 he, Pete Boardman and Dick Renshaw had been avalanched above the Shoulder. In similar conditions they had battled their way down in little or no visibility. With three men it had been a desperate struggle for survival. Now Michel was having to do the same thing on his own, for he had already told Benoît that he had found no sign of Maurice and Liliane.

In subdued tones we talked to the Italians, everyone half-listening to the hiss of static from the radio, aware of any slight fluctuation of signal. Then it clicked open, and a faint gasping voice announced itself, "Ici Michel, ici Michel . . ."

Benoît leapt for the radio and there followed a conversation that, without understanding all of it, I will always remember. Benoît with the laconic cool of an air traffic controller talking to the pilot of a stricken airliner, was giving detailed and precise instructions to Michel about route finding.

"Keep right, keep right, don't veer to the left, then straight down for perhaps two, three hundred metres . . . over."

The panting, weakened voice of Michel asked for more details. The conversation was made all the more moving by the total control on both sides. Finally with typical French formality Michel signed off, "Merci bien, Benoît, à bientôt."

Benoît replaced the radio on the table and turned to us. "He has perhaps a fifty-fifty chance that he finds the ropes. If not . . ." he shrugged his shoulders.

Oh God, I'm going to cry, I thought, and stared hard at the floor. No-one spoke for a few minutes.

The afternoon passed with more coffee and more calls from Michel, whose voice was weaker with each transmission. Benoît patiently explained what details he could to Michel. The problem was, of course, that Benoît could only guess where Michel was and, despite having descended the same ground so recently, could merely give a general description of the topography. He thought that when Michel reached the top of the sérac barrier he would be able to tell the difference as he

109

approached, by the updraught of wind and a change of texture in the snow. But there was also a danger of hidden crevasses as well as the awful thought that he could fall straight over the top.

As dusk fell the radio opened once more. Michel's voice seemed stronger. Benoît was suddenly more animated and turned to us. "He has found piss stains in the snow." Cheers and whoops of relief filled the tent. Three thousand metres above us in the driving murk Michel heard them on his radio. Now with the knowledge that he was still on the route, his chances of finding the top of the fixed ropes were much higher.

Wending our way back across La Manche to our tents as dusk fell, I reflected on how wrong it is to stereotype other nationalities. All Frenchmen are not volatile, emotional, prone to panic in a crisis, as those calm and precise conversations had just witnessed. I felt drained. "I can't be doing with another day like that," I muttered to Jim Hargreaves as we arrived home. Even though Michel's prospects were far brighter now than they had been, I couldn't help feeling that he was still not out of the wood. Wanda and the two Basques, being lower than Michel, were presumably well on their way down by now. The next day was uneventful. There was no more news from Michel until late the following morning. He had descended as far as Camp 2 below House's Chimney, arriving exhausted in the dark, and had then slept for over twelve hours.

It was still difficult to accept that Maurice and Liliane were dead. The last time I had seen them they had seemed so optimistic, Maurice very determined on his seventh expedition to Pakistan, Liliane with designs on soloing Broad Peak as well as climbing K2. Walking past the French tents, it was hard to realise that Maurice and Liliane, like John and Alan, would not be coming back. Their Liaison Officer was genuinely upset and showed me a letter that had arrived by mail runner that morning. Addressed to Maurice, it was from Madame Barrard, his mother. "Poor fellow. Now he will not be reading this letter." Despite stating the obvious, the sentiment was heartfelt and I could only nod agreement.

I had been concerned in the last days

about my role as film-maker and, more specifically, the sending of the ITN news reports. Initially I had only filmed our own expedition, but the events of the last week were going to hit the headlines whatever I did. On none of my previous expeditions had there been any conflict of interest between my roles as climber, film-maker or news reporter. I had never given much thought to the possible problems that could arise. Now I had to decide where my own priorities lay and examine my conscience concerning what and how I filmed. It would have been very easy to record Michel's radio calls, for instance. I had a Professional Walkman in my rucksack outside the tent at the time. But I felt that my involvement was one of personal concern and friendship and there was just no way that I could have recorded what might have been Michel's last words. A professional reporter would no doubt have seen this as a lost opportunity and an unprofessional attitude but I couldn't bring myself to treat a human drama as a piece of titillating news. (Later John Barry told me he would have stopped me if I had tried!) But it was also clear that I had a duty to report the details of the accidents as accurately as possible. All sorts of criteria of bad taste, sensationalism and intrusiveness, suddenly became terribly important to sort out to my own satisfaction. I had not been at Base Camp for Alan's funeral and my relief at missing it was undoubtedly due in part to having avoided the problem of whether or not to film it. Everything in me told me I shouldn't, indeed couldn't, but I could see that in six months' time it could be, in the right context, a moving and valid scene in the documentary film. A small part of me wished I was more ruthless, but a much larger part was glad I wasn't.

However, the arrival in Base Camp of Wanda and Michel would be different. It would be an emotional but happy event and I hoped that I would be there to film it. On the morning that I assumed they would be returning, I went over to the Strip and wandered up to the far end to chat to Norman Dyhrenfurth. Various porters were coming and going along the moraine leading to Advance Base Camp and I failed to register the approach of the two small figures, vaguely assuming from their frail appearance and because both were wearing flamboyant Pakistani silk scarves, that they were two of the Polish girls who had recently arrived. As they drew abreast they stopped.

"'Allo, Jim." It was Michel, with Benoît who had gone to Advance Base to meet him. Michel's face was haggard with sadness and exhaustion. I put an arm round his shoulders, fighting unsuccessfully to hold back the tears.

"God, Michel, don't do that again, please." It was a banal comment but I couldn't think of anything else to say.

"Too many mistakes . . . too much time . . . we spent too long too high up." Michel spoke softly, half to himself.

I steeled myself. "Michel, I'm really sorry about Maurice and Liliane."

Michel looked at me with a sudden intensity. "No, no, you must not give up hope. Maurice is strong, he will come down I am sure!"

Once more I could not reply, but wondered if Michel had clung to what was by now a non-existent hope as a way of willing himself down.

A few minutes behind him came Wanda

The Trango Towers. The Nameless Tower is
the separate rock to the right. Uli Biaho, banded
by cloud, is to the left. *(Brian Hall)*

West Face of Gasherbrum IV, from Gore. *(Michel Parmentier)*

Maurice and Liliane Barrard, the husband and wife team who climbed the Abruzzi Ridge with Wanda Rutkiewicz and Michel Parmentier, only to be lost on the descent.
(Michel Parmentier)

Al Rouse, apostle of alpine-style climbing, had an obsession with K2 and the motivation to achieve the summit.
(Jim Curran)

Wanda Rutkiewicz had already climbed Nanga Parbat and Everest and was to be the first woman on the summit of K2.
(Jim Curran)

Benoît Chamoux on his return from a record setting twenty-three-hour ascent of the Abruzzi. *(Jim Curran)*

Above, Chogolisa. Twenty-nine years earlier Kurt Diemberger (right) had attempted it with Hermann Buhl after their first ascent of Broad Peak. Buhl fell to his death from the South-East Ridge. In 1986 Diemberger was filming on K2 with his partner, Julie Tullis (left). But both had summit ambitions. *(Jim Curran)*

Avalanche at Base Camp. *(Jim Curran)*

Jim Curran filming Aid Burgess on the fixed ropes below Camp 1 on the North-West Ridge. *(Jim Curran)*

Jim Curran's high point on the mixed face between
Camps 1 and 2, the Savoia Glacier below. *(Dave Wilkinson)*

Goretta and
Renato Casarotto
(Goretta Casarotto)

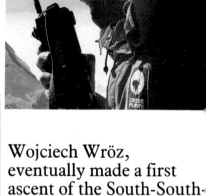

The most impressive
climbing being done on K2
was Renato Casarotto's
attempt to solo the Magic
Line. After this radio call
he gave up and descended
the fixed ropes to his
death in a crevasse fall.
(Krystyna Palmowska)

Wojciech Wröz,
eventually made a first
ascent of the South-South-
West Ridge with Piasecki
and Bozik. *(Jim Curran)*

Tadeusz Piotrowski,
as I remembered
him in 1977 in the
Kishtwar Himalaya.
He made a first ascent
of the South Face
with Kukuczka.
(Paul Nunn)

Phil Burke jumaring on the North-West Ridge.
(Al Rouse)

Michel Parmentier on his return to Base Camp after an epic solo descent from the summit. *(Jim Curran)*

Benoît Chamoux near the summit of Broad Peak. *(Benoît Chamoux)*

The summit of K2 and the Bottleneck seen from the Shoulder. *(Benoît Chamoux)*

with the American doctor Steve Boyer carrying her rucksack. She looked years older and like Michel her face had caved in. As she passed the American tents Chelsea greeted her and I filmed the smiles and tears as they embraced. Suddenly they were surrounded by members of almost every expedition, greeting them and leading them back to their tents for long overdue meals and sleep. Wanda had frostbitten fingers, not too bad but needing attention, which was given by Steve. It was not until the following day that we found out any more of what had happened.

They had, as Michel had said, been very, very slow. They had spent nights at 6300, 7100, 7700, 7900 and 8300 metres on the ascent, the last a bivouac in a tent but without sleeping bags. On the morning of 23rd June they left for the summit early, but the Barrards and Michel stopped for a rest and a brew just short of the top. Wanda continued above and reached the summit at around 10.30, the others about 11.00. They all stayed on the summit until around midday. Incredibly, they could only descend to their last bivouac site at

8300 metres, still, of course, with no sleeping bags. Meanwhile Mari Abrego and Josema Casimiro reached the top at around two p.m. and descended without incident to their top camp at 8000 metres. Maurice had been very tired and he and Liliane had been the last to leave the tent on the morning of the 24th. It had been windy with poor visibility. The three most likely possibilities were that Maurice and Liliane had wandered off route and got into an irreversible position, or that in their fatigue they had simply fallen off, or that they had collapsed through exhaustion and died. Whatever had happened, they had pushed themselves too hard on the ascent and, given the small height gains on the last three days, had been unwise to carry on.

Michel and Al talked at length about the importance of spending as little time as possible above 8000 metres. It was an almost obsessive article of faith with Al, who was acutely conscious of the damage that the body can incur from a prolonged stay so high. Deterioration both physical and possibly mental is rapid at that altitude. Even with good supplies of gas (for melting snow to make drinks) the body is still deteriorating fast. With only a third of the oxygen in the atmosphere that there is at sea level to support life, and the increased strain on the heart and lungs, even resting is of dubious worth. The Barrards seemingly were not going as well as Wanda or Michel. I wondered if Maurice, who had appeared to be the strongest of the four, had exhausted himself in his efforts to help Liliane. He had seemed desperately keen for her to be the first woman to climb K2 and I had often thought that it was potentially dangerous for a husband and wife team to climb together with so much at stake for each partner, so much extra strain on decision-making.

As for Wanda and Michel the tragedy seemed to have put them further apart and they could barely now speak to each other. Michel was very concerned about Maurice's mother, who was old and had a weak heart. He feared the loss of her son would destroy her. He was also worried about legal and insurance problems. The lost money at the airport weighed heavily with him. He was anxious that if anyone found Maurice's body they should photograph it, for French insurance companies could be awkward if firm evidence of death was not provided.

Wanda, whose frostbitten fingers were obviously very painful, seemed to be out of touch with reality, already planning to climb Broad Peak, which in her present condition she was not fit for. Even if she recovered physically, which at K2 Base Camp seemed unlikely, she would be risking much worse frostbite. She sounded vague, irrational, and quite obsessed with 8000-metre peaks. I wondered if she was planning to do the grand slam of all fourteen for, with Everest, K2 and Nanga Parbat ticked off, she had certainly got three of the most difficult out of the way, and she was going to Makalu in the autumn. I wondered if Steve Boyer would discourage her from attempting Broad Peak so soon. But she appeared to be trying to persuade him to climb it with her! However, I remained in awe of the strength, skill and determination of the first woman to climb K2, and amazed that the experience had not left her, temporarily at least, satisfied. Perhaps at that level she, like so many other top climbers and adventurers, would never really remain fulfilled for long and would always be driven to seek out the next challenge.

6

THE last mail run had brought us long overdue letters from wives, girlfriends and, in my case, daughters. Gemma and Becky had been in the same class at the same school as Nick Estcourt's two sons, Matthew and Tom, and had terrible memories of the pain and sorrow the boys had undergone when Nick had been killed on K2. Understandably they were never wildly enthusiastic about my expeditions, despite my frequent reassurances that as a cameraman and coward I was in relatively little danger. K2 of all mountains was the one they feared most and the fact that I was on it must have been a constant worry for them both. But their letters were always entertaining, treasured and frequently reread.

Also in the mail were two letters that posed problems. John Porter and Jim Hargreaves had job or business commitments that were becoming more and more pressing. John had always thought that the expedition would last about two months and he and Bev had planned on sixty days' food at Base Camp. But John had not really taken into account all the time spent in Islamabad, Skardu and the walk-in and was becoming concerned that he stood a very good chance of being sacked if he did not return to work on time. Now a letter from his girlfriend Rosie (now his wife) confirmed that if he were late he would be in deep trouble. With the weather showing no signs of improving, John wrestled with dates and times that would give him as long as possible on the mountain. Jim too was worrying about his prolonged absence from home and the many problems that would await him on his return. He had done a superb job in organising the practical day-to-day machinery of the expedition, so good that it was now running itself. So he resolved to walk out with John when his time was up. John's impending departure would bring the climbing team down to six, but it also deprived Al of a compatible partner and perhaps the most sympathetic ear he had.

For Al was becoming increasingly beleaguered. The twins were always diplomatic and unwilling to be drawn into arguments, but John Barry and Phil Burke gradually became implacably opposed to virtually everything Al suggested. I found Al intensely irritating at times. He unwittingly presented an air of superiority and, at times, conceit in his own considerable past successes, and the entertainment value of the Rouse Factor was wearing thin. But he, more than anyone on the expedition, had an awesome determination to climb K2 and the self-confidence that he was capable of it, though this had to be constantly reaffirmed by reminiscing about past achievements. John and Phil seemed more and more uncertain of their chances, yet more and more dogmatic and argumentative as a result.

I felt for Phil who seemed to find it very difficult to pace himself. Attempting to keep up with the Burgess twins, he found the effort shattering every time he gained altitude for the first time, though on his second attempt he would cruise the same ground. But it had always seemed very unlikely that Phil, on his first Himalayan expedition, would climb K2 by a new and difficult route without oxygen. I wondered if he understood the enormity of what he clearly felt to be a realistic ambition. "If I don't personally climb K2 I will consider the expedition to be a failure," he had said before leaving England and I felt that by setting his sights so high he was courting disappointment.

John, also, seemed over-ambitious. At forty-two he had only a couple of Himalayan expeditions behind him and was short on high-altitude experience. Despite his massive physical strength and bulldog determination, he had acclimatised slowly. I felt that neither of them stood a real chance of climbing K2 and wished that they could see that, and adopt a more positive supporting role. As it was, any of Al's plans that didn't seem to give them an equal chance of being at the front were heavily criticised. Dave Wilkinson normally kept quiet and didn't enter into the controversies. He seemed content to carry loads day after day, gradually increasing his fitness, stamina and acclimatisation. The twins, who tended to measure achievement in terms of speed alone, may not have been very impressed, but I thought that Dave could yet come good and surprise everyone.

Al's throat infection was still giving cause for concern. It was not improving, despite antibiotics, and Steve Boyer's help with a steam ventilator. Despite his capacity to infuriate everyone, I felt terribly sorry for Al as he privately admitted to me that he had doubts whether he would be able to carry on. He had been given a hard time by all of us and now he could see that if John Porter was to go he would almost certainly be unable to compete with the twins who would inevitably team up at some point in the near future.

Apart from his throat, Al felt well-acclimatised and still strong. Knowing how much this expedition meant to him and knowing his worries for the future, I hoped that somehow he could gain some real satisfaction from the expedition. At one stage, when he was feeling more than usually pessimistic, he seemed quite keen to get more involved in the film. He, along with John Barry and John Porter, had already shot quite a lot of Super 8 footage and was more enthusiastic about getting good quality movie footage than still photography. But I doubted if he would really get any long-term satisfaction from the film. Al was first, last and always a climber: everything else paled into insignificance.

At last on 30th June the weather showed some signs of improving. We all resolved to go back up the following morning, but John Porter's time was almost up. He had been banking on one last attempt if it looked as though a summit bid was a realistic proposition. But with all the new snow that had fallen, it seemed that we would either need a much longer period of fine weather than we had ever experienced, or that we would have to make two attempts. Either way John's chances of the top were minimal and he recognised this. He had to go at least to Advance Base to pick up some personal gear, and would leave the day after with Jim.

We went over to the Strip to say our goodbyes to the Americans and to Michel Parmentier who would have left before we returned. In a few short weeks, we had got to know them well. The Basque pair, Mari Abrego and Josema Casimiro, were also leaving, apparently "under arrest" for an illicit ascent of the Abruzzi, but more likely as a golden opportunity for Casarotto's Liaison Officer to get back to Islamabad, for he was to accompany them. Jim Hargreaves and I went to their tent where Michel joined us. Goretta had made a cake that would have graced any Italian *pasticceria*, and Renato had opened a bottle, heavily disguised in its wrapping, but undoubtedly containing whisky. Mari and Josema both had frostbitten fingers: could the whisky have been medicinal to help the circulation? It certainly helped ours and the afternoon quickly degenerated into a jovial and mildly drunken party. Liaison Officers from other expeditions came and went, often, to my amusement, furtively sipping the whisky themselves. Renato and Goretta presided over the festivities before slipping away after about half an hour. Once again the image of knights in shining armour came to mind, for there was something in their demeanour that suggested a bygone age of courtliness and gallantry. Jim and I gradually waxed emotionally, if not eloquently, into a "go for it" mood, before making our own farewells.

Michel in particular had become a close friend to all of us. He wished us luck and confessed that he would be much happier if everyone was returning with him. I knew that, unlike many fleeting friendships made in the mountains, this one would be renewed.

We all set out early the next morning, except Al and Dave who would now be climbing together. Al had decided to spend two days getting to Camp 1 to give his throat a chance to clear up, and was not going to leave until the afternoon. I also would take two days, but preferred to get to Advance Base as early as possible. This time, feeling far fitter, I managed to arrive there just as the others, who had stopped for a rest, were setting off for Camp 1. By now, though it was not yet nine a.m., the sun was up and shortly the Savoia Glacier would warm up like a greenhouse. John Barry tried to persuade me to carry on, but I preferred to conserve my energy. I made a drink while John Porter got his gear together, close to tears of disappointment as the decisive moment arrived when he would return to Base Camp. There was not a cloud in the sky and it was obvious that settled weather had at last arrived, at least for a few days. John was racked with doubts about his decision and even at this stage seemed on the verge of changing his mind. But eventually he got up ready to go.

"See you in a few weeks, then."

"Have a good walk-out. Give Cass a ring when you get back."

John pushed off with his ski sticks and skied off, a lonely figure against the white glare of the glacier.

The effect of the sun melting the ice around the tents at Advance Base had stranded them, high, if not dry, and the floor of the biggest tent was uneven. Since it had not been used to sleep in for weeks, except occasionally by me, it was chaotic inside. I tried to get some semblance of order and sort out food, drink and brewing materials. Then, before it was too late, open every available vent and put sleeping bags across the roof, in the vain hope of keeping the inside tolerably cool. What it must be like to spend an entire expedition with a Base Camp on the Savoia Glacier I dreaded to think. I felt like an ant in a pudding basin. Even inside the tent the heat was appalling. Outside the ice had turned to slush and squalid dirty puddles formed in which bits of rubbish floated. The day crawled past (I had forgotten to bring a book) broken by bouts of extreme energy as I lit the stove or collected water or changed position in the tent. Each action demanded an incredible amount of willpower and left me gasping for air.

Late afternoon, and within ten minutes the raging heat faded through pleasant cool (about two minutes), to chilly, to ice cold. Outside the tent the West Face of K2 was immense and brooding. Harmless puffy clouds drifted across the summit as the shadows lengthened. Down the glacier a small figure breasted the last steep rise and approached.

"Oh, what ho, J.C."

It was the standard Rouse greeting, slightly surprised and normally accompanied by a wide grin. Al often affected this parody of the public school, Cambridge undergraduate, perhaps because he always claimed that his years at Cambridge had been unfulfilling and that socially he had found the place difficult to cope with. But there was always an element of the student in Al, even the schoolboy, and it was not hard to see him as the bespectacled fourth form swot.

On our own, Al and I always picked up the threads of a long friendship. We could confide in each other, he his fears and doubts about the expedition, the climbing, even his future life; me the problems of the film. Neither of us could do much to help, except listen, but it probably did us both good. We sorted out the chaos in the tent to enable Al to lie flat, and started the evening meal as dusk fell.

"I hope Wilkie's all right. What time did he say he was going to leave?"

"About half four I think, he'll probably arrive when the meal's ready."

Dave, as if on cue, did just that and got comfortably ensconced in the adjacent tent into which we could pass him food and brews.

Next morning promised a slight novelty. Instead of skiing up almost to the foot of the Savoia Saddle we were trying out a new route that the twins, John and Phil had discovered. This left the glacier basin much earlier and traversed up to the right to reach Camp 1, bypassing the fixed ropes (which in any case were now needed higher up). This variation enabled the whole journey to be done on skis. Skinning on the hard frozen snow in the shadows of dawn was very satisfying, as was the speed at which I was going compared with two weeks before. At last I felt I was beginning to acclimatise and get a bit fitter.

As I gained height I could look across at the Savoia Saddle from a different angle. It was always a puzzle to me why the Americans in 1975 had gone to the Saddle. For it was self-evident that the pinnacles above would be difficult and time-consuming, but even more obvious that it added at least another half mile onto what was already an immensely long route. When H. Adams Carter and Bob Bates had reconnoitred the Savoia they had recommended the route that we were now following (and that the Poles had followed). But their advice had been ignored, seemingly in favour of the hidden ramp behind the pinnacles which had proved to be non-existent. Even odder, I thought, for a day up to the Saddle would have shown that, and nothing would have been lost in changing the route. Pondering this academic point was as good a way of passing the time as any, and soon I found to my surprise that the tents of Camp 1 were in sight only some 200 metres away. But the last half hour was in the sun and within minutes I was reduced to a drunken stagger, collapsing in a heap outside the tents and needing a long rest before getting myself together to melt snow for a much-needed drink.

Al Burgess and John had already departed for Camp 2. Phil and Aid were to follow them and Al Rouse and Dave were to do a carry up to 2 before going up to stay. I had by now psyched myself up to getting up the ropes to Camp 2. I dearly wanted to see across into China and film the progress on the upper section of the ridge. I planned to take a sack of camera, film, sleeping bag, and personal gear to the halfway point on the fixed ropes, a prominent arête easily visible from Camp 1, then come down, have a rest day and return quickly, I hoped, to the sack and try and make it to Camp 2 (6800 metres). It seemed a realistic ambition. Whether or not I could then get any higher was obviously a moot point. The 7000-metre barrier was still beckoning and if I was ever going to get there I stood as good a chance now as I ever would.

Sharing a tent with Al I made an early start and was able, plodding slowly and deliberately, to walk up the narrow valley to below the bergschrund and the beginning of the fixed ropes. As dawn broke the others caught me up but I had time to film them, dark silhouettes against the first rays of sunlight hitting the Savoia peaks across the glacier. As I fumbled with crampon straps they swept past and up the frozen avalanche debris to the bergschrund, before moving swiftly up the fixed ropes. Everyone seemed to be going like steam trains at over 6000 metres, without showing any sign of altitude at all. Clipping my jumars onto the first fixed rope dangling down the steep rear wall of the bergschrund, I realised that I was actually doing something that could loosely be described as climbing. Admittedly it only involved putting one foot in front of the other and sliding the jumars up the rope, but the first long rope-length was impressively steep.

The others soon disappeared round a corner and I was left, going at my own pace and working out how to conserve energy, change from one rope to the next at the end of each rope-length and the best line to choose to avoid the rope snagging on rocks. Engrossed with the unaccustomed activity, I realised that I was actually enjoying myself and, as the views changed by the rope-length, it was easy to feel a sense of achievement that had been lacking in the confines of the Savoia Glacier. I progressed slowly but reasonably steadily until, just below the prominent arête that was my target for the day, the first rays of sun caught me. Almost instantly I was reduced to a crawl. The last two rope-lengths took about as long as all the preceding ones and the last twenty metres, up the very crest of the arête to a small ledge and out under a rock wall, were shattering. At last I made it and clipped my sack onto the pegs with a sigh of relief.

I had broken my previous height record of 6500 metres (on Kongur in 1981) and had good reason to feel pleased as I gazed out at the immense vista. Just for today I could reasonably claim to be climbing K2. The summit of Angel Peak, now not much higher, thrust gracefully above the West Ridge over to views which I could now see of what I took to be Masherbrum and, in the far distance, Paiju. I stayed for about twenty minutes, hoping that I would see Al or Dave on their return journey and be able to film them, but there was no sign. It was only ten a.m. but already intolerably hot. Fearful of falling stones from above, I decided not to wait any longer and, making sure that the sack was anchored securely out of harm's way, I set off down on the first abseil, marvelling, as always, at how with gravity on your side, distances shrink dramatically. In no time at all I was back at the bergschrund and stomping down the last slope to retrieve my ski sticks for the last walk through slushy snow back to Camp 1. Behind me Al was now in sight and catching me up and I went as quickly as I could to get a brew on before he arrived.

Because of his throat, Al had been nursing himself but, even so, I was surprised that he and Dave were now opting for a rest day. High above at Camp 2 progress was slow with the accumulation of new snow since the last attempt. It had been a desperate job merely breaking trail to the bottom of the fixed ropes, and a "Camp 2½" had been put in at the top of the snowslope to save both time and effort. Uncovering the ropes was proving a grim struggle: the first time John had reached the bottom rope he had had trouble even finding it, buried under a metre of new snow, and when dug out it was encrusted in ice. Despite the perfect weather which had now lasted four days, our high point was still a long way above. Though it was an unspoken thought, it was beginning to dawn on me for the first time that the odds on our getting up the ridge were lengthening.

We spent the rest day repitching tents, chatting and filming. John had heroically carried my big tripod to Camp 1 on his last trip which meant that I could get high quality telephoto shots of the ridge. I always found rest days a problem. Looking forward to them was one thing, but as soon as they started there was a "back to work tomorrow" feeling as the day sped by all too quickly. I planned to make a really early start at first light. If I was going well I might be able to reach the ridge and Camp 2 before the sun hit the upper slope of the face.

Despite having been halfway before I was even more apprehensive than the first time and found sleep hard to come by. I tried not to disturb Al and I made a brew and got ready to go. Unencumbered by a sack I made good time and by the light of my headtorch picked my way in the dark up towards the start of the ropes. Suddenly the still of the night was broken by a loud crash and rumble of an avalanche. A moment's horror, then relief, as I realised it came from the end of the cwm and that a rock fall had come down from the colossal buttress at its head. But I was shaken and felt suddenly lonely as I approached the bergschrund.

Something seemed to have changed and I looked in vain for the end of the fixed rope. Had it been avalanched? Above the ice slope was swept bare and polished. I felt vulnerable and very lonely standing on avalanche debris in the dark with God knows what above me that might possibly detach itself at any moment. Suddenly in despair and disgust I made the decision to go down and returned to Camp 1 just as Dave and Al were preparing to leave. Convinced that an avalanche had swept away at least the first rope-length I urged them to take axes with them. When they had left, I miserably retreated to the tent for a brew and a doze.

I was in a quandary and hoped I could sort something out on the evening radio call, but this was thwarted by flat batteries and I could make no contact with either Bev, by now on his own at Base Camp, or Al at Camp 2. But not long after I was surprised and slightly dismayed to see a figure descending. Who could it be and what had happened? It was Phil. He looked shattered and his face was pinched and drawn.

"I had a desperate night at 2½—hallucinations, puking, spent most of the night outside the tent convinced I was going to die. Aid slept right through it."

He had felt so bad that there had seemed little point in him staying up to recover, but I noticed that Phil had brought all his personal gear down with him which boded ill. Was he resigned to giving up the North-West Ridge?

"I think J.B. will be down in the morning if he doesn't feel any better. He's absolutely shagged as well."

Pondering this news I almost forgot to ask Phil about the ropes. When I did he looked puzzled.

"I've just come down them. They're exactly the same as they always were."

Suddenly it dawned on me what I had done and I felt acutely embarrassed. I had somehow in the dark taken the wrong line up to the bergschrund, arriving some fifty metres to the left of the line of the ropes, and in the direct line of an old avalanche chute that had almost filled in the bergschrund. I felt ashamed of such an elementary route-finding error.

That night, before I went to sleep I again wondered what to do next, for if John did descend in the morning it would only leave four climbers on the ridge, surely too few in the conditions Phil had described to make any significant progress. I was also beginning to feel the strain of constantly moving around the mountain on my own. If John and Phil were to go back to Base Camp, perhaps it would be sensible to go with them, for now the others might well be pushing up the ropes and Camp 2 might be empty.

John did descend the next morning, arriving tired and disillusioned at Camp 1 where he described how he felt about fixed-rope expeditioning. The analogies he drew were unprintable but heartfelt. He was utterly frustrated with the lack of progress and whatever the outcome, needed at least two or three days' rest at Base Camp before he could even think about another attempt.

This put me in an even bigger quandary, for now I had to try and read the future. My camera and personal gear were effectively stranded; abandoned, even, if I didn't go back, yet by now the prospect of staying up and then descending to Base Camp on my own was frankly terrifying. Skiing down to Advance Base was far steeper than anything I'd done before and man-eating crevasses were opening up by the day.

"John, I hate to ask you this, but if I

come down with you will you give me a skiing lesson?"

"Course I will, mate. No problem."

Musing that this could possibly be a world high-altitude record for ski instruction we set off. Under John's expert tuition I learned more about skiing in the following hour than in all the misspent time I had wasted previously. Still carrying a heavy sack, I found it terribly hard to turn but at last, zig-zagging across the glacier above Advance Base and doing the most elementary snow-plough turns at the end of each zig (or zag), I could appreciate for the first time that skiing could be fun. I was also aware that virtually every skier in the world would give their right arm to be in such magnificent surroundings. I really was incredibly lucky.

Hot and sweating we stopped at Advance Base for a drink and a rest. Suddenly in a flurry of snow the twins arrived out of the blue. What had happened?

"That's it, we've given up on the ridge."

"Oh?"

"We're going on the Abruzzi instead."
"Oh!"

The previous day Aid had reclimbed the fixed ropes to the high point, often laybacking on them to pull them clear, and had managed to fix one more rope-length to 7400 metres. It had taken almost a week to regain the previous high point and yet again the good weather was showing signs of coming to an end. The twins had broken the news to Al Rouse and Dave. Presented with a fait accompli they could only acquiesce. I admired the twins' decisiveness. In not prolonging the agony they had left us with a chance of an alternative, but I was personally disappointed suddenly to find that all my efforts to get to Camp 2 were in vain. My immediate worry, that I would either have to go back up the ropes for the camera or abandon it, were alleviated when Al, carrying a monster load, brought it back to Camp 1. He and Dave were also on their way down.

And so, out of the blue, all our hopes and plans for the North-West Ridge were dashed. Everyone had worked hard but with only six active climbers the route was just too big an undertaking. The weather had been appalling and there seemed no sign of any long settled spell. On this, my third trip to the Karakoram, I was not particularly surprised, for neither of the previous expeditions had been any better. But it was frustrating to know that there had been summers (of which 1985 was the last) with up to three weeks' continuous fine weather. There was no doubt in my mind that, had we had such a spell, we could have almost certainly got up the ridge. But it was with a feeling of huge anticlimax that I followed the others back to Base Camp, conscious that if they were to make an attempt on the Abruzzi, I would be playing no part in it.

7

THE Abruzzi Ridge seen from our Base Camp was once described by Al as "the longest slope in the world" and when layers of cloud swirled around it, revealing and concealing sections, it did look interminable. Apart from an early reconnaissance by Conway in 1892, and the first serious attempt on K2 in 1902, when Oskar Eckenstein and the infamous Aleister Crowley attempted the North-East Ridge, every single expedition to the mountain had attempted the Abruzzi Ridge until the American North-West Ridge Expedition in 1975. Crowley (otherwise known as the Great Beast 666 or even the Wickedest Man in the World, from his fascination with drugs, sex and black magic) had in his youth been a mountaineer of great judgement. He had spotted the possibility of climbing the South-East Ridge but had been overruled by the others in favour of the North-East Ridge. Had they attempted it, the ridge might well be known now as the Aleister Crowley Ridge!

But despite Crowley's opinion being confirmed by the subsequent climbing consensus, the Abruzzi Ridge is no push-over. Even in 1980 Pete Boardman, Joe Tasker and Dick Renshaw were still impressed by the technical difficulties, particularly on the Black Pyramid below the Shoulder, finding the climbing far harder than they had expected. They came away with renewed respect for the pre-war pioneers of the Abruzzi, such as the Americans, Wiessner, House, Houston, Bates and Wolfe, reckoning that they were climbing at a far higher standard than the equivalent British expeditions on Everest.

It had taken five expeditions before an Italian team led by Ardito Desio finally climbed the mountain by the Abruzzi Ridge in 1954. It was a large nationalistic expedition run very much on the same lines as the successful 1953 British Everest expedition. Lino Lacedelli and Achille Compagnoni were the summiteers. The expedition lost Mario Puchoz early on from what would now be diagnosed as pulmonary oedema, but was then thought to be pneumonia. On the summit bid, Walter Bonatti, in support of the two lead climbers, had undergone a forced bivouac on the Shoulder with the Hunza high-altitude porter, Mahdi, from which they were lucky to survive. But it had otherwise been a textbook ascent, learning from the experience of previous expeditions.

The Abruzzi had already had its share of epics and disasters. In 1938 Charles Houston had led a (for the time) remarkably small expedition and reached the top of the Shoulder at the base of the summit pyramid. The following year Fritz H. Wiessner, a German-born naturalised American, had followed in Houston's footsteps, leading a ten-man expedition with nine Sherpas. Nine camps were made before Wiessner and Sherpa Pasang Dawa Lama came within a whisker of climbing K2. Wiessner got to about 8400 metres, just below the final easy-angled summit slopes, when Pasang refused to pay out any more rope, fearing they would be benighted on the summit and beset by evil spirits. They lost their crampons on the descent to Camp 9, which stopped another attempt the following day. In continuing perfect weather, a rarity on K2 at such an altitude, they tried again the day after, before accepting that cramponless it was impossible.

Then followed a series of misunderstandings that culminated in an appalling tragedy. Dudley Wolfe was a young millionaire playboy whose mountaineering experience was limited to guided ascents in the Alps. But he had proved surprisingly strong and determined on his first expedition and was at Camp 8 just below the Shoulder. Unknown to him the camps below were being systematically stripped of sleeping bags by the Sherpas, who were apparently under the impression that the summit had been reached. Wiessner and Pasang descended to Wolfe and they all decided to descend to Camp 7 to reprovision before another attempt. Wiessner left his sleeping bag at Camp 8. On the descent the inexperienced Wolfe stepped on the rope and all three fell, sliding helplessly towards the monster drop down to the Godwin Austen Glacier before providentially hitting a patch of soft snow and slithering to a halt just in time.

At Camp 7 they discovered the camp

had been abandoned and the sleeping bags gone. Wolfe's sleeping bag had been lost in the fall and only Pasang had one. After a terrible night, Wiessner and Pasang descended, but Wolfe decided to wait for them at Camp 7, using Pasang's sleeping bag. They discovered to their horror that Camp 6 was also abandoned, and as they descended, so were all the other camps.

From Base Camp a desperate rescue bid was mounted by the Sherpas, all the Americans by now being too exhausted to reascend. Three of them, Kikuli, Kitar and Pinso, eventually reached Wolfe who was still stranded in Camp 7. He was too weak and apathetic to move, and was lying in a mess of food and his own excrement. He could only say that he would try to get down the following day and refused to read a note sent by Wiessner. The three Sherpas descended to Camp 6 where a fourth Sherpa, Tsering, was waiting.

Unbelievably, after a day of storm, the three set off yet again in a forlorn attempt to get Wolfe down, or at least get him to sign a note exonerating them from further responsibility. They never returned and no light has ever been shed on what happened to them, or to Dudley Wolfe.

The next attempt on K2 was not until 1953. Charles Houston returned to the fray, again with Bob Bates and also George Bell, Bob Craig, Art Gilkey, Dee Molenaar, Pete Schoening and British army officer Tony Streather, whose role as Transport Officer rapidly developed into that of a full climbing member. It is often assumed that alpine-style climbing has only been practised in the last ten years or so, but there are examples of small light-weight expeditions succeeding on high mountains that go back to the turn of the century. Tom Longstaff's ascent of Trisul, Smythe and Shipton's ascent of Kamet and Tilman and Odell's conquest of Nanda Devi spring to mind. Houston's two K2 expeditions were also fine examples of small cohesive units attempting to climb the mountain in the best possible style of the day. Houston's 1953 expedition was certainly small compared with John Hunt's successful Everest expedition a few months earlier.

It arrived at Base Camp in late June and by the beginning of August the whole team was poised at Camp 7 (7700 metres) for the first summit attempt. Then a violent and prolonged storm moved in. Houston and Bell's tent was wrecked on the fourth night. Seemingly oblivious to the danger they were in, they read, wrote diaries, and Dee Molenaar painted watercolours. It was not until 6th August that retreat was even discussed. But on the 7th the gravity of the situation was suddenly brought home to them when Art Gilkey developed thrombophlebitis: blood clotting in the veins of his left leg. Though Gilkey was effectively doomed from that moment, the others resolved to try and effect what would have been the most desperate and unlikely mountain rescue of all time: to stretcher and lower Gilkey down the Abruzzi Ridge. But it was not until 10th August that the weather improved enough to allow the seven exhausted men to start the herculean task.

Faced with dangerous avalanche-prone slopes, they started the interminable descent, lowering Art Gilkey through the storm. After hours of nerve-racking, strength-sapping and highly dangerous manoeuvring of the makeshift stretcher the unthinkable happened. George Bell slipped and one by one the others were dragged after him. In the ensuing tangle of bodies and ropes Pete Schoening managed to stop the fall with some unbelievably quick thinking and expert belaying. A shocked, injured, concussed and frostbitten team managed to find their way to a makeshift campsite. While preparing the ledge and pitching the tents, Gilkey was anchored securely by two ice axes some fifty metres away in a gully. When Bob Bates, Bob Craig and Tony Streather returned to collect him, the gully was bare. Art Gilkey had been swept away in an avalanche. There was no sign of the axes which had been ripped out.

Gilkey's death may well have saved the others, who nevertheless still had the most gruelling and nightmarish descent to complete. It took another three days to reach safety. How long it would have taken with Gilkey is a matter for conjecture. Houston's team erected a memorial cairn to him before starting the long journey home. The following year Desio's expedition succeeded at last.

But it is Houston's expedition that still

fires the imagination. Jim Wickwire, who in 1978 made the first American ascent of K2, wrote of his own expedition's achievement in the context of 1953. "Somehow reaching the summit of K2 seemed less important than the magnificent efforts of all who had preceded us." 1953 was summed up memorably by Charles Houston: "We entered the expedition as strangers but we left it as brothers."

Thirty-three years later at our Base Camp under the Gilkey memorial, I feared that with our expedition the reverse would be the case. Our attempts on the North-West Ridge had fizzled out with the knowledge that we had not even managed a summit bid. Given the weather and the weakened team we should have had no reason to reproach ourselves, let alone blame anyone, but by now no-one was particularly happy with themselves, or with others. It was 8th July and after six and a half weeks at Base Camp, we were having to start all over again.

Attempting the Abruzzi presented an instant problem. We hadn't got permission. But neither, to all practical purposes, did we have a Liaison Officer any more. Lieut. Agha had become more and more of a trial as the weeks passed, alienating everyone by his arrogance and obstructiveness, and embarrassing the other Liaison Officers on the Strip. He had reached the point of demanding the right to censor our mail and had by now moved his tent over to the Strip, so he was barely on speaking terms with any of us. Bev thought he was near to a breakdown and had no hesitation in writing a note to that effect that would give Agha some justification for going. If he knew we were attempting the Abruzzi he would certainly forbid it outright. However, we hoped that other Liaison Officers on the Strip might be more understanding.

Everyone agreed that to pack up and go would be an admission of total failure. A quick ascent of the Abruzzi would, we felt, still be second best, but better than nothing. But it would have to be done with some care and sensitivity for, on one side, we risked the wrath of other expeditions and the outright refusal of their Liaison Officers to let us carry on and, on the other, the possibility of being fined or charged another peak fee by the Ministry of Tourism. It seemed unfair that the peak fee had effectively become a *route* fee on K2 when in the past, and still on other Karakoram peaks, it had been a blanket permission for the whole mountain. But we would be prepared to pay up if we succeeded. To have to fork out an extra 2000 dollars, having failed, was something none of us wanted.

I didn't relish the prospect of all the deception involved for if we were to attempt the Abruzzi as a cloak-and-dagger job, I would have to keep well away. For me to be seen on the lower reaches with a camera and tripod (assuming I ever retrieved them from Camp 1) would be blatantly advertising our intentions and would leave the Liaison Officers with no alternative but to stop us. We had a hunch that they would turn a blind eye so long as no-one lodged a protest, or we didn't ask them directly, for we were not the first that year to change our plans. The two Basques had clearly flouted the regulations, as had Herrligkoffer's expedition. We still weren't sure whether or not the Italians really had had permission to switch routes from the South-South-West

Ridge and it suited us to assume they hadn't.

Licking our wounds at Base Camp, with the weather yet again breaking down, it was time to catch up with current events from the Strip. The big news was that six members of the Italian Quota 8000 expedition had climbed K2. They were Gianni Calcagno, Tullio Vidoni, Soro Dorotei and Martino Moretti, Jozef Rakoncaj and Benoît Chamoux. Jozef Rakoncaj, a Czech climber, had previously climbed the North Ridge of K2 in 1983, also with an Italian expedition. Success on the Abruzzi meant that Jozef became the first person to climb K2 twice. But the event that really caused raised eyebrows was that the Frenchman, Benoît Chamoux, had climbed the Abruzzi in *only twenty-three hours!* "Gobsmacked" was the only word to describe our reactions. Benoît had already climbed Broad Peak in under a day, before his first attempt, when he met Michel at the beginning of the storm. He was obviously perfectly acclimatised and supremely fit. Also he was travelling unladen and following, not breaking, trail.

Even so it was an incredible achievement, almost unthinkable only a few years ago.

Le sportif is the name given by the French to what English-speaking countries might loosely describe as "speed climbing". It is so far very much a continental phenomenon, first manifesting itself in the Alps with rapid solo ascents of classic routes, two or three or more north faces in a day, with helicopters or sometimes even hang-gliders to get from one route to another. The emphasis is on the individual superstar in terms of sponsorship and media attention. So far *le sportif* has had little attention or understanding in the British climbing press, and its exponents seem to us to be participating in an almost alien activity. Our admiration for Benoît's feat was real enough but it was hard, if not impossible, to compare what he had done with what Renato Casarotto was trying to do. In our eyes Renato's dogged and prolonged sorties on his self-imposed task of solo-ing the unclimbed South-South-West Ridge were almost beyond praise and we could accept Renato into our more traditional concept of what climbing was about. Benoît seemed to be turning tradition inside out.

Al, having congratulated him on his success, invited Benoît to come over to Scotland in the winter for some ice climbing. Benoît looked apologetic and said he didn't think he would be good enough to do the hard routes, explaining that he was not really a technical climber. Everyone metaphorically heaved a collective sigh of relief. That he could be out-climbed and out-bouldered meant he was not that good after all. The fact that he had just succeeded in doing in a day what we had manifestly failed to do in six weeks was conveniently forgotten.

The departure of the Americans and Michel was only compensated for by the presence of the Koreans and Poles. The Koreans were incredibly friendly, polite and hospitable. Their Base Camp tent even had a video (solar-powered, of course) and on an early visit John Barry and I were invited in to watch a film. Wondering what it would be, we were amazed to find it was a documentary about—I could hardly believe—K2! The incongruity of watching a climbing film with the real thing just outside the tent seemed lost on the Koreans. As we sat and watched, we sipped various concoctions of tea. These, the Koreans explained, with much recourse to graphic gestures to illustrate the point, were supposed to be aphrodisiac. Just what I really wanted, I thought gloomily, sat in sub-zero temperatures in an all-male society in a tent somewhere in Central Asia, watching a climbing film in Korean.

A constant problem with the Koreans was their use of and comprehension of English. Many of them spoke it quite well but didn't seem to understand much of what we said. Thus a simple question like, "How many porters did you have?" would be answered by, "Ah, I am thirty-three years old." I think they couldn't bear to admit to us that they couldn't understand and felt it impolite not to answer. It made for some hilarious misunderstandings.

The Poles quickly took over from the Americans as being the most obviously friendly expedition. Many British climbers feel an affinity with Polish and Czech climbers and there has always been a strong rapport between the climbing communities. Janusz Majer, the leader, was dark-haired, stocky, with twinkling eyes and a big black beard. He and Al got on instantly. Wojciech Wröz was, we all thought, a real star. A slightly cynical view of life and a studied air of nonchalant detachment, plus a sharp sense of humour, made him an instant favourite. He was very good looking, and puffing his short, stubby pipe, his eyes would crease in amusement at some secret thought, then with a cutting phrase he would have everyone in hoots of laughter. I could imagine him as a schoolmaster being hero-worshipped by the boys and drooled over by the girls.

I vaguely thought I had met him before but couldn't place him until he told me that he remembered meeting me in Skardu with Joe Brown, Mo Anthoine and Martin Boysen, whom he reminded me of in mannerisms. It was 1976 and we were off to attempt Trango Tower when he had been with Janusz Kurczab's Polish expedition to the North-East Ridge of K2. He had returned again to the North-West Ridge in 1982. Each time he had nearly reached the summit, could he be third time lucky?

The two other men with them were Przemyslaw Piasecki and a Czechoslovakian "guest", Peter Bozik. Neither spoke much, if any, English and were harder to get to know. An "Independent Ladies Team" were with them though I couldn't see how or why they were so named unless it was for the convenience of the Polish media, for they all climbed and lived together with no sign whatever of being anything other than one harmonious whole. The girls were well-known and experienced Karakoram climbers, Anna Czerwinska, Krystyna Palmowska, and Dobroslawa Miodowicz-Wolf. Krystyna spoke fluent English (the best of the whole team). The girls were small and first impressions were certainly not of super-human strength or great athletic prowess. But they were all going well and carrying heavy loads up the fixed ropes above the Negrotto Col. Their young Liaison Officer was very much a part of their team, and a stark contrast with Agha, who was by now desperate to go home. It was about the only thing on which we all agreed!

The stormy weather continued and by 9th July we were all mildly concerned for the welfare of those still on the mountain. Kurt and Julie, who had been filming the Italian's summit bid were still somewhere high on K2. They had, we understood, made an unsuccessful summit bid but were not yet down. Casarotto was still up and also missing were the two Poles, Jerzy Kukuczka and Tadeusz Piotrowski, who had come with Dr. Herrligkoffer's expedition. I felt a twinge of guilty embarrassment about Tadeusz. Before we had gone up for our last attempt on the ridge we had visited the Poles who had just arrived. In the corner of the tent was a big bald man in his mid-forties with a huge red beard who looked like a Cézanne self-portrait. Whenever I glanced in his direction, I imagined that he was staring at me. As with Wojciech, I had the feeling that I had seen him before but it was not until I was halfway back to our Base Camp that the penny dropped. In 1977 I had been on an expedition to Barnaj II in Kashmir with, among others, Paul Nunn and Geoff Tier. Tadeusz Piotrowski had been camping on the grass in front of the government rest house at Kishtwar before going off to attempt a solo ascent of the Brammah peaks. We had had a splendidly boozy evening with him and the next day I had driven him in our expedition van to the roadhead from which his walk-in started. Now I had failed to recognise him, though in fairness he had lost most of his hair and his beard was far bigger. Also, of course, he probably wasn't too sure about me. I looked forward to meeting him again and hoped that he and Kukuczka had either climbed their route or managed to retreat in the worsening weather.

Jerzy Kukuczka was a name that was rapidly acquiring international status, for he had suddenly emerged as a potential challenger to Reinhold Messner in the race for the fourteen 8000-metre peaks. With K2 Kukuczka would have bagged his eleventh, only one behind Messner, who still needed Lhotse and Makalu to complete the list. (This Messner achieved in autumn 1986.) Many of Kukuczka's ascents however were by new and difficult routes, whereas Messner had tended to solo the easiest route available. Once again comparisons are fairly meaningless. There are so many variables in Himalayan climbing, unlike athletics, that no two ascents are ever comparable. It was obvious that Piotrowski and Kukuczka were a formidable team, and from what we could gather, were at, or near, the top of their route.

Events on the mountain were so complex that it was some time before we realised that Beda Furster and Rolf Zemp, who had originally been with Piotrowski and Kukuczka as part of the Herrligkoffer expedition, had switched to the Abruzzi and had actually climbed it on the same day as the Italians and Benoît. Meanwhile, Dr. Herrligkoffer and Doris Kustermann, having been flown in to Broad Peak Base Camp, had quickly developed symptoms of pulmonary oedema and been flown out again, apparently only just in time. Norman Dyhrenfurth referred to him as "Dr. Herrlicopter" as a result!

I felt a twinge of disappointment that I had come so close to the legendary doctor but had not met him. He remained in my mind a rather sinister enigma: an old man whose life had been dominated by mountains yet who had never been able to go above Base Camp; a man who despite his organisational experience, attracted feuds and controversy on almost every venture; and a man whose whole concept of leadership and power seemed to be profoundly at odds with the people who continually placed themselves under his command. Did he, I wondered, actually enjoy the mountains in the same way that I did? Did he enjoy the company of climbers? Was he still acting out some strange ritual that had to do with atoning for the loss at a formative age of his step-brother and hero, Willy Merkl, in an appalling and protracted disaster on Nanga Parbat in 1934? Questions that had no easy answers. But I would have liked to have actually seen him.

On the evening of the 10th we were all invited over for dinner with the Italians. We arrived in the dusk and found our way through the little hamlet of tents to the big communal North Star tent.

"Bloody hell, they've even got street lights!"

Sure enough their solar-powered electric lights actually extended to one slung between the tents. Inside, a delicious array of dried meats and spaghetti and sauces awaited us, as well as the welcome news that Kurt and Julie had returned safely. As we started the first course they came in looking utterly shattered. Kurt, who arrived first, told us that he thought they had been a bit lucky to get away with it. Then Julie pushed through the door of the tent.

"It's good to see you down in one piece," I said, and meant it.

"You didn't imagine we wouldn't get down, did you?" was the disconcerting reply.

Hmm, I thought.

They had spent ten days away, climbing and filming up to 8000 metres, then spent 6th July attempting the summit, reaching 8300 metres above the Bottleneck Couloir before being unable to complete the difficult leftward traverse that leads eventually out onto the summit slopes. Kurt had had trouble in getting pegs into the friable rock and ice and without decent belays they felt it was too dangerous to continue. They had given up around four p.m. but had waited another day, before starting their retreat on the 8th in ever-worsening weather. It was at about this time that the leader of the Austrian team, Alfred Imitzer, had made an unsuccessful solo summit bid. Their descent on the 9th-10th had been a battle, and it showed in their faces. Whether or not they would have the strength for another attempt seemed a moot point.

The evening was relaxed and enjoyable. The Italian leader, Agostino da Polenza, was well known to everyone who had been on Everest with Al in the winter of 1980-1, for he had been attempting Lhotse at the same time. I liked all the Italians and regretted the language barrier that separated us.

On 13th July Dave Wilkinson and I did the round of the Strip. At the far end I renewed my acquaintance with Norman Dyhrenfurth, apologising to him that our last meeting had been abruptly curtailed by the return of Michel Parmentier. We chatted about recent events, then I asked him if Tadeusz Piotrowski was down yet. He looked at me aghast.

"You mean you haven't heard? He's dead."

Shocked once more, but somehow

accommodating the news more readily this time, we asked what had happened.

Piotrowski and Kukuczka had set off on 4th July and, making good progress, established a camp at 8200 metres on the 7th below a twenty-five-metre rock step that would bring them out into the upper summit snowfields of the Abruzzi. It had taken the whole day to climb the step, with Kukuczka leading, as he had done throughout the climb. They abandoned their tent, sleeping bags and stove and the following day (8th July) reached the summit in high winds and poor visibility. They had bivouacked again at 8300 metres and on 9th July descended to the bottom of the Shoulder. On the morning of the 10th (now without fluids, food or shelter for almost three days) they tried to find their way to the site of the Korean Camp 3 and the end of the fixed ropes. Piotrowski was climbing behind Kukuczka who, crossing the top of the Gilkey Couloir, felt something hit him. It was one of Piotrowski's crampons and as Kukuczka turned to look, the other one also slid past him. Piotrowski attempted to stop himself with his ice axe but suddenly fell past

Kukuczka and out of sight. Numbed by the accident Kukuczka managed to reach the Korean Camp and descended safely to Base Camp on the evening of the 12th.

It seemed clear that the accident had been caused primarily by exhaustion, and Tadeusz presumably not putting his crampons on correctly. Even with ski-type "instant" bindings it is still easy to make a mistake if the boots are heavily iced up, and Piotrowski by this time must have been numb with cold and fatigue. I was amazed at the Poles' achievement but also at how far out on a limb they were prepared to go to reach the summit. No stove, no sleeping bag, and no tent seemed to me pushing their luck too far.

Jerzy Kukuczka was sitting outside his tent as we passed and we stopped to give him muted congratulations and condolences. He had mildly frostbitten feet and hands but still seemed remarkably strong and fit looking, given what he had just been through. Compared to Michel and Wanda he looked as though he could do it again tomorrow and I began to realise the magnitude of his achievements. In stature he reminded me slightly of Pete

Boardman, who was also very powerfully built.

On our way back we decided to call in on Renato and Goretta, approaching their tent slightly cautiously in case we might be intruding on their privacy. But Renato seemed pleased to see us. By now he had been to 8200 metres twice, each time retreating in the face of bad weather. The strain of his lonely adventure was telling and he confessed he had been worried about his mental state on his last attempt. He and Goretta had moved their tent up the Strip so that Goretta could be nearer other expeditions' Base Camps and have more company when Renato was on the mountain. As before, the tent was scrupulously tidy and organised.

Renato showed us a French book of their abortive attempt on the South-South-West Ridge in 1979 and planted a stubby finger at his high point, tantalisingly close to the summit. He said his next attempt would definitely be his last and that he couldn't wait to go home. While Goretta once again fed us drinks and cakes, he thumbed through photos and magazine articles about K2. He was still brimming with an enthusiasm and love of mountains, despite his setbacks, and he still looked remarkably well. Presumably, I said, amidst laughter, the result of Goretta feeding him good food. As we left we wished him luck on his last attempt and shook hands. I noticed, as I tried not to wince in his powerful grip, that he and Goretta both seemed to avoid the sun, she, as always, in the white floppy sunhat and huge dark glasses, he in jacket and salopettes. Despite his dark hair, his skin was still quite pale.

Dave and I returned across La Manche, which in mid-July was becoming a raging torrent, to Base Camp where the others received the news of Piotrowski's death with resignation. Five lives lost since we arrived. Not much to say and even less to do, but privately worry and question the futility of pitting ourselves against the indifferent monster. But still, despite the deaths, each evening K2 had the power to compel and fascinate as streamers of snow blew out into space from the summit rocks high above.

8

AT last Agha was going back to Skardu, to everyone's great relief. He had tried to patch up his differences with us and departed on reasonable terms. Despite everything, it was hard not to feel sorry for him, for the whole experience must have been one long trauma and might have repercussions on his future army career. He left carrying an enormous sack and taking two porters with him, similarly laden. He hired another almost as soon as he was out of sight, and cadged a lift on a helicopter for some of the return journey.

The helicopters were a new phenomenon for me. In 1976 and '78 they were almost unknown except in dire emergency. But now, with the dispute over the frontier, two large army bases had been established, one near Gore campsite, not far from the Mustagh Tower, and another at Concordia. Helicopters did a regular shuttle between the two, and in and out of

Skardu. They were still only to be called for in an emergency by climbers and trekkers, and before leaving Islamabad we had paid a large bond to cover the cost of such a flight which, if not used, would be reclaimable on our return. But it seemed that with the right contacts and enough money, they *could* be used for purposes other than rescue: Dr. Herrligkoffer had been flown *in* as well as out. Operating perilously close to their height ceiling, they would land with rotor-blades beating at full power, stay with engine running for only a minute or two and take off with a roar and whine as they fought to gain height in the thin air, before careering off, still only metres above the séracs of the Godwin Austen Glacier, down to Concordia. Peace and quiet would descend once more. I always found the helicopters disturbing. Even when only visiting, as they sometimes did, the associations of mountain rescue and accidents were never far away.

But at least their presence meant that the weather was not too bad, and any portent of good weather would be seized on as we waited in increasing frustration for a chance to attempt the Abruzzi. K2 and the Karakoram are supposed not to get the monsoon. That's the theory, but in my own limited experience the arrival of the torrential storms and floods in the plains of the Punjab is invariably followed by bad weather in the mountains. At Base Camp, looking south beyond Chogolisa, the sky was almost always filled with a high line of clouds that even in good weather would recede but never totally disappear. With the onset of bad weather it would advance. If it was not the fringe of the monsoon I would be interested to know what it actually was. For days now the weather had been unsettled and a collective despondency hit us and those on the Strip who had still to climb their various routes. The only slight consolation was the knowledge that in these conditions, our decision to abandon the North-West Ridge was certainly the correct one.

At last on 15th July it looked good enough to give the Abruzzi Ridge a go. Phil summed up the mood of the climbers about the change of route.

"In the North-West Ridge we had a

very remote, very large objective which needed a very big team. We gave it the best we'd got, considering that two members dropped out. I think time is now running out for us. If we're going to reach the summit of this mountain, I think we ought to do it in good style on the Abruzzi, alpine-style climbing. Half a dozen of us —just go for it."

Al was confident they could achieve it in four days. "We'll carry four days' food on our backs, and a small amount of rope, about 300 feet between us, a few carabiners—a very small amount really, about the same as you'd take on an easy climb in the Alps."

Everyone set off in ones and twos, not in the best of tempers, because we had got ourselves embroiled in a breakfast argument about ordering porters for the walk-out, scheduled for 28th July. Bev and I were left behind meanwhile to ward off any inquisitions from Liaison Officers or others who would, inevitably, find out fairly quickly what was going on. The previous day Dave Wilkinson had discovered that, by staying on the near side of La Manche, they could keep out of sight of the Base Camp tents on the Strip until well past them. It all seemed a bit like playing at cowboys and Indians and I couldn't help feeling that, should anyone catch them sneaking past, they could look both foolish and in the wrong.

The rest of the day passed uneventfully and the following morning seemed quite encouraging as well. They had obviously not been sent back and until midday the weather held up. But then clouds and wind yet again appeared from nowhere, and as the afternoon passed the Abruzzi slowly disappeared into a lowering, though broken, cloud ceiling. From Base Camp it looked mediocre but no worse, so it was with some surprise that Bev and I, who had gone for an evening stroll out on to the glacier, returned to see two figures by the tents.

"Hell, it's the twins—why are they back so soon?"

While a huge meal was being prepared, Aid and Al explained what had happened. The previous day they had walked up to the Advance Base at the foot of the Abruzzi and had stopped for a brew with the Koreans, who were occupying it, before pressing on to Camp 1 with no problems or comments from them. Camp 1 was deserted and they slept in tents that had already been pitched by Koreans and Austrians, being careful not to use or disturb their contents. Everyone was very aware that not only should the team *be* completely self-contained, but they should be *seen* to be so, otherwise any objections raised would be all too justified. But at Camp 1 there seemed little point in digging out fresh tent platforms next to empty tents.

Next morning the twins had set off early, followed by Al and Dave, then Phil and John. Aid and Al jumared swiftly up the continuous line of ropes and climbed a wire ladder hanging down a steep buttress out of the line of an avalanche-prone gully close to the Austrians' Camp 2, immediately below House's Chimney. This famous feature, first climbed in 1938 by William House, is normally iced up and must have once been quite a tour-de-force to ascend. Now it is permanently festooned with fixed ropes or wire ladders, and is merely a high altitude *via ferrata*. Above the chimney easy snowslopes led to the Korean Camp 2. The twins, climbing strongly, carried on up the Black Pyramid where they overtook an Austrian party that included Willi Bauer. The Austrians, obviously impressed at the turn of speed the twins were showing, asked them if they intended to go to the summit that day! But soon afterwards it began snowing lightly and the temperature dropped abruptly.

Below, Al Rouse stopped and was given a hot drink by some Korean high-altitude porters at their Camp 2. Dave, who was going somewhat more slowly, almost caught him up before he set off once more. Nearer Camp 3 than Camp 2 Al stopped to put his down suit on. Dave caught him up and did likewise. They were debating whether or not to carry on when the twins reappeared out of the mist, descending rapidly. To go down now would mean that they could get back to Base Camp the same day and be ready for another attempt.

As if to confirm their decision the Austrians, too, were descending. In the end everyone came down and, as usual, the twins were the first back, the others coming in as the light faded. Phil had managed to get badly sunburnt feet on a sunny day at Base Camp and was in agony going downhill.

It had been a long day for everyone and Dave was last in. Returning through the tents of the Strip (for by now there was no point in hiding), he had been accosted by Julie Tullis who was, Dave told us in his matter of fact way, "in a bit of a flap". She explained that Renato Casarotto, who was descending the South-South-West Ridge, had fallen into a crevasse. She wanted to borrow a headtorch as she and Kurt were going up the Filippi Glacier below the slopes of the Negrotto Col to rescue him. He had radioed Goretta at Base Camp for help and was apparently unharmed, but possibly suffering from hypothermia. Dave seemed to think that it was all under control and, assuming that everything was well in hand, we went to bed as soon as the meal was finished.

I had hardly gone to sleep, or so it seemed, when I was woken by shouting and immediately knew that it meant trouble. Lying in my bag, staring into the dark, I could just hear Wanda's voice urgently talking to Bev. For a few minutes, still warm and not fully awake, I tried to pretend that it would all go away. Then a voice, I think it was Aid Burgess, was raised.

"Come on, lads, we've got to lend a hand with Casarotto."

An hour later we assembled in the Austrians' Base Camp tent, the one that had been cordoned off, and it was the first time I had been inside. Julie was back, having come down with Wanda after helping get Renato out of the crevasse. The help was being mustered to bring him down. Now Julie was busy handing out mugs of coffee.

"It's really *very* good of you all to come," she said, unintentionally making it sound as if we'd been invited for afternoon tea at the vicarage, "but I don't think it's really necessary, we've asked for a helicopter to arrive at first light."

Surely if it was serious enough to warrant a helicopter, I thought, the more help the better, and could Julie really believe that, even in good weather, a helicopter would arrive on time as requested in this part of the world. Bev pointed out that even if it did, more damage could be caused in the first few minutes of a helicopter rescue, unless the casualty was properly prepared to be lifted.

Kurt and one of the successful Italian summiteers, Gianni Calcagno, were still up on the glacier. Renato we were told was suffering from hypothermia and possibly minor injuries. Warm clothes and a stove seemed to be priorities, but we also picked up an oxygen set from the Koreans.

As we set off we passed the Casarottos' tent and heard Goretta's choked and tearful voice asking Julie what was happening. In the dark there was no chance of following the easiest line up the steep moraine that leads onto the Filippi Glacier and we floundered about on loose scree, panting and cursing. The first complex section of the glacier was a small rickety icefall. In the dark it seemed horrifying, with black drops all around, as we picked our way cautiously through the maze. Bev, Phil and I were roped together and near the top Phil warned me urgently about a dodgy step across a snow bridge.

"Don't stand on it. Jump!"

I hesitated, misunderstood his instructions and jumped too early, landing at the very point Phil had told me to avoid. I crashed through the bridge but Phil held me while I scrabbled, panic-stricken, to safety, to be given a well-deserved lecture. Shortly afterwards the icefall eased off into an easy-angled slope and we could move together freely.

About fifty metres above a group of figures was gathered in the darkness, head-torches flashing and casting long shadows. There was something almost sinister about the little gathering, like medieval conspirators hatching a plot in some black and white horror movie. I dreaded what I would find, for as I approached I could sense more than see a dark shape at their feet.

"Get Bev up here, we need a second opinion."

That's it, I thought, all urgency suddenly evaporating. Bev passed me and knelt down beside the form. Beneath a sleeping bag a plastic boot protruded. Bev carefully carried out his examination before replacing the bag, and in a choked voice confirmed what we already knew. I averted my eyes, not before seeing Renato's strong white forearm, jersey sleeves still rolled up. I remembered, when shaking hands only days ago, the strength of his grip. The arm was still pale, the strength gone. Next to me Wanda wept quietly. Tears filled my eyes but I was too numb to cry.

We had brought up a spare radio and, knowing that Agostino would be waiting with an open line at Base Camp, we passed it to Gianni who, composing himself for a moment, reported that Renato was dead. Sobbing, Agostino asked him to call again in ten minutes when he had broken the news to Goretta. Standing in the cold with the first slight indications of dawn in the sky, we shared out chocolate and cold but heavily sweetened drinks from our water bottles, talking in hushed tones about what to do next. The choice was brutally simple: either carry Renato down, which with the glacier in its present state would be a long, complex and possibly dangerous business, or lower him back into the crevasse from which he had been rescued. Everyone favoured the latter as being the less painful for Goretta and all concerned, but she would have to be asked first and would hardly be in a fit state to make such a decision.

At last Agostino opened up and Gianni put the alternatives to him. Once more Agostino went away to consult. It was growing lighter by the minute. A grey overcast dawn revealed a poignant sight. A line of tracks led, seemingly unbroken, straight into the crevasse. Closer inspection showed that the far edge had collapsed under Renato's weight. The utter futility of it all struck us forcibly. How could we justify our ephemeral pleasures in the mountains when this could so easily be the result? I resolved never to travel unroped on the Savoia, or indeed any other glacier, again. Nine years ago, a friend, Don Morrison, had died in almost identical circumstances. Had I learned nothing from his death? For I had skied and walked on my own on the Savoia for two months. The still dark shape could so easily have been me. A man admired by us all in the prime of his life had, after enduring heaven only knows what privations as he battled with himself and the mountain, died within minutes of safety on ground that every other expedition had walked across every day without giving it a second thought.

Agostino came on the air again. Gianni listened intently. Goretta had agreed to Renato's burial up here but wanted to come up to make her final farewells. So Gianni remained behind while the rest of us began the descent which seemed far shorter and easier in daylight and in only ten minutes we were unroping at the edge of the glacier.

Everyone started down the long scree slope but I noticed Kurt was still slowly removing his crampons. It seemed callous to rush off and I asked him if he would like me to go down with him, which he readily agreed to. Slowly and methodically the "old man of the mountains" moved down placing his feet carefully at each step and using next to no energy. His brown lined face was pained and he looked very tired after his long vigil.

"I just cannot understand it," he kept repeating. "Renato was a careful climber, not some young kid. Why did he do this thing?" Kurt's thick Austrian accent was heavy with sadness as he told me the heart-breaking details of the last twelve hours.

Late the previous afternoon he had been watching a figure just visible from Base Camp descending from the Negrotto Col. As it approached the last broken area of glacier it suddenly disappeared. Kurt said he was almost instantly certain that it had fallen down a crevasse. Who was it? Casarotto seemed the most likely but it could have been one of the Poles, also on the same route. He had strolled across to Goretta and inquired whether she knew of her husband's whereabouts. Goretta had told him that Renato was indeed descending but she didn't think he would be very far down, certainly not as far as the glacier. She mentioned that he was due for a radio call but he was late. Fearing the worst, Kurt stayed with her and a few minutes later, Renato's voice came over the radio.

"Goretta I have fallen . . . I am dying . . . please send help quickly."

Gianni, Kurt, Wanda and Julie all ascended to the crevasse. Renato had fallen forty metres, but, still conscious, had radioed frequently to Goretta. They found him sitting at the bottom of the crevasse with little obvious sign of injury, but he told Kurt that he had lost all feeling and that his head was cold. Having arranged a pulley system, Kurt said that initially Renato had been able to help himself out, but after only a few metres had sagged back on the rope. At the top he had collapsed unconscious and died very shortly afterwards, presumably of massive internal injuries, or possibly a broken spine. As Kurt told the story, he kept asking himself why Renato had been crossing the glacier at that time of day, when the snow was at its most dangerous.

"If he had waited, maybe two hours, it would have been okay. How can he do such a thing?"

As we reached the foot of the scree slopes, there was a traverse around a deep glacier pool. Kurt urged me to take good care, explaining that once he had fallen in a similar one head first. Carrying a heavy rucksack which had flipped over his head, he had only avoided drowning with the help of his companions, who had seen him fall. It seemed more of an indication of Kurt's state of mind than any particular danger, I thought, as we slowly walked back down to the Strip. On the way we met Agostino who greeted Kurt with silent but heartfelt emotion. Goretta, who was in no fit state to move, had changed her mind about going up. I was relieved that she was to be spared, but Kurt was not so sure, saying that death was easier to come to terms with if you have seen the body. As we approached Base Camp we looked back to see two tiny figures standing side by side with a small dark horizontal shape between them. As we reached Base Camp I turned and looked once more. Now there were only two figures. Renato had been returned to his crevasse. Removed as I was from the scene, the tears fell silently but freely.

9

NEXT day I walked over to the Strip to try and retrieve various bits and pieces of equipment we had loaned the others on the rescue. I avoided Kurt and Julie's tent for I knew Goretta was with them, but Kurt called me over as he had collected all our gear. I mumbled my condolences to Goretta, lost for words. Goretta sat, very dignified and collected, arm in arm with Julie. Bev had removed Renato's watch to bring down to Goretta. She had it on now; with the metal strap far too big for her, she was wearing it almost around her elbow.

"Please thank your friends for trying to help to save my husband."

Needless to say the promised helicopter had not arrived but one was still expected to take Goretta back to Skardu. I hoped for her sake it came quickly. The Italians were leaving, as had Norman Dyhrenfurth and the remnants of the Herrligkoffer expedition, and at last Wanda decided to go as well. She had given up her ambitions for Broad Peak.

"Too many friends have died."

The Strip was beginning to look slightly forlorn as frame tents which had become landmarks disappeared. We saw more and more of the Polish expedition who had all come down in the bad weather. Anna Czerwinska later wrote about the death of Casarotto: "We started getting the impression that we were participants in some mysterious drama, and that something was happening that was beyond normal statistics and chance." Words which summed up the feelings of most of us. Though sixteen people had so far climbed the mountain, there did seem to be a jinx on expeditions to K2 this season. Was there any way of exorcising it? Or was it just a series of wrong decisions?

Krystyna Palmowska told us that on his last bid Renato had gone up to 7100 metres before once again the weather turned. At about the same time as everyone had retreated on the Abruzzi, Renato had made a long radio call to Goretta, weighing up the pros and cons of continuing. Krystyna said she thought he was in a desperate quandary. To admit defeat would be a colossal blow to his ego and pride.

Earlier he had told the Poles: "It's a wonderful route. If I reach the summit I shall give up my solo climbing."

They had asked him why, when he had come so near, he had twice retreated. He had replied: "The climb is hard from the first to the last metre. The day when I shall be trying to reach the top, the weather must be ideal because I don't want any extra risk."

At the end of that long radio conversation with Goretta, Renato had come to his decision and Krystyna said that she felt that he collapsed psychologically and almost physically before her eyes. All his hopes and dreams were shattered and he had descended "almost in a trance" at high speed.

Later Al and Aid Burgess reminisced about their first meeting with Renato in Peru in 1977. He had been climbing on the North Pillar of Huascaran, soloing as usual, a huge rotten overhanging buttress, while they were climbing a nearby ridge. A colossal avalanche had swept the North

Face, and when it cleared they had shouted across, fearing the worst. But Renato's answering call was, as Al said, more than just a reply.

"From then on we felt we knew him and were sharing the same experience."

Renato had completed his climb slightly before the twins, who followed his tracks down the following morning. To their surprise they found that they led straight over an eight-metre high ice wall.

"We couldn't understand it and peered over the edge—sure enough there were two huge footprints at the bottom! He'd either fallen over in the dark, or jumped and misjudged the distance. But a few metres further on he'd gone into a hidden crevasse and thrown himself forward and managed to scramble out on the far side. We didn't see him again until K2 Base Camp, but we always remembered that one shouted conversation across the face."

Perhaps this time Renato, in his disappointment and obvious desire to get back to Goretta as quickly as possible, had relaxed his guard just a bit too soon. But maybe he also had, as is not uncommon in top mountaineers, a slightly casual attitude to the dangers of easy ground. I had noticed this before. On the Kongur expedition, for instance, the climbers were always reluctant to rope up on the featureless Koksel Basin below the South Ridge of Kongur which was seamed with huge hidden crevasses. And on this trip everyone seemed very blasé about the Savoia Glacier.

The effect of Casarotto's death on us was difficult to assess. The other fatalities had been tragic events but remote, as if they had happened on another mountain. Now it had come very close to home. Though we hardly discussed it, unspoken thoughts hung heavily in the atmosphere. I wondered if it would be the last straw for some, if not all of us. Phil Burke seemed to be on the verge of going anyway; he had received a letter from his bank manager politely asking him if he would be going back to work in the near future. Al Burgess had arranged to meet up with his girlfriend in Srinagar at the beginning of August to go trekking in Kashmir, before travelling on to Nepal and Everest where he would be guiding a client. Aid, too, was fretting, for Lorna, his wife, was meeting him in England on 12th August to walk the Pennine Way. John Barry also had commitments and was increasingly worried about earning a living. Only Dave Wilkinson and I, both polytechnic lecturers, could stay on through the August summer holiday, and of course for Al the thought of going home unsuccessful was almost too much to bear.

On the morning of 20th July, Phil and Al Burgess decided to leave. Phil was quite hollow-cheeked, with legs like match sticks, after the efforts of the last two months, and he joked that he would be light enough to get back into rock climbing at his normally very high standard. But he must have been bitterly disappointed that the trip was ending on such a low note. As for Al, he, like Aid, was philosophical. He had his trek, then Everest, to look forward to, and after that more mountains.

I was impressed with their attitude, for in a way the Burgesses were only competitive with themselves. They were utterly content to be in mountains, particularly in Nepal where they had almost become honorary Sherpas. A conversation with Al Rouse shortly before they left was revealing. The twins both claimed that walking or climbing on any terrain, scree, ice, rock, snow, was an activity they took positive delight in doing rhythmically and well. Al professed to loathe everything except extreme rock climbing and regarded Himalayan climbing as an activity to be endured rather than enjoyed. But Al had the willpower to put up with all the suffering. Because the Burgesses didn't suffer much, perhaps, I thought, they didn't need much willpower? With Phil and Al's departure the climbing team was down to four.

Later the same day, Al Rouse and I visited the Strip. As if there wasn't enough bad news, this time we learned that Liliane Barrard's body had been found near the bottom of the huge avalanche cones above the Godwin Austen Glacier, about halfway to Advance Base on the Abruzzi. She had fallen a colossal 3000 metres. There had been no signs of Maurice. Another pall of gloom descended on the Strip.

Still no helicopter for Goretta. Al and I discussed events with Kurt and Julie, with Goretta looking on silently. Before we left

Al nervously steeled himself and spoke to Goretta.

"I just wanted you to know how much we all liked and respected Renato. He was an incredible man. All of us thought that he was doing the best climbing of anyone on K2 this year. We're all very, very sorry."

Goretta wept openly and embraced us both as we parted. I was proud of Al, it was a very moving little speech and came from his heart and I knew how difficult it had been for him to make.

The next morning we heard at last the faint drone and chatter of a helicopter and a few minutes later saw it coming up from Concordia, as usual only just clearing the glacier, to land on the Strip. Without any discussion we all stood on the crest of moraine by the tents in a ragged line. The helicopter lifted off and as it flew past we waved our goodbyes to Goretta. I don't suppose she noticed.

In the afternoon I went with John and Aid to take a succession of black and white photographs for an instructional book John was doing on ice climbing. They spent a couple of hours front-pointing up, down and sideways on the steep ice of a sérac. In the middle we were distracted by the grim sight of a long procession of climbers and porters carrying Liliane's body down the Strip and over to the Gilkey memorial. It was another harrowing image that, with a telephoto lens, would have been a graphic picture for a colour supplement. But I couldn't take it and was once again relieved that we were far enough away not to get involved.

However, a couple of days later I went up to the memorial cairn with the vague feeling that perhaps I ought to. It was a curiously moving spot. Inscriptions had been hammered out on aluminium saucepan lids to the memory of those who have perished on K2. In the dry pollution-free atmosphere, they all looked as though they had been completed the day before. Gilkey, Puchoz, Al Pennington, the Barrards . . . with a sudden jolt of recognition I noticed that Nick Estcourt's plaque was also placed on the cairn. I thought that it had been left on the rocks of the West Ridge; then I remembered that Pete Boardman, Joe Tasker and Doug Scott had been back to attempt the ridge in 1980 and had presumably thought it too remote a spot and had brought it here. It had been hammered out by Captain Shafiq, their Liaison Officer, and was strangely but emotionally worded and spelt: "In the memory of great hero who has sacrificed his life for the great cause of mountaineering God may rest his soul in peace !Amin! Late Mr. Nick Estcort."

I stood and looked at the Abruzzi. A good viewpoint, K2 one way and Chogolisa the other and Broad Peak in between. Despite its remoteness, in the middle of Central Asia it was still a special place to be remembered in.

I descended to Base Camp and looked back up at the cairn. Two figures were there, and in the afternoon light it made a quite acceptable shot for the film. Seen through the zoom lens, I realised it was Kurt and Julie. They also were filming the cairn and then turned their camera to our Base Camp.

"You can be in my film if I can be in yours!" I shouted.

Laughing, they too came down for a brew and a chat. Julie was still shaken by the death of Casarotto and the strain of looking after Goretta. She said, rather unconvincingly I thought, that she had given up any hopes of climbing K2, but they had to stay longer to finish their film. In any case they had left some camera equipment at Camp 2 and would have to return to get it. I took this as a coded way of saying that they were keeping their options open. Kurt I noticed, did not comment and I wondered how determined he was. Even now they both looked very tired and they seemed to spend hours sleeping each day. Recovery at Base Camp after a prolonged stay at 8000 metres could only be partial. At forty-seven and fifty-four it seemed slightly unrealistic to expect them to recover enough for another attempt.

Julie appeared keen to get back to England. Her autobiography was due to be published shortly and she and Kurt then had another filming commitment in China. She also had a series of lectures to give in the autumn which she hadn't prepared. I found the last reason mildly amusing as my own preparations for lectures never take more than a couple of hours. Julie looked a bit taken aback by this, but I explained I had a slight advantage. What was that? she enquired. I'm a lecturer! Finally Julie simply confessed she had been away for far too long and was homesick. I wondered if, given a really good spell of weather, she would change her mind.

Both Kurt and Julie had what seemed to me to be a romantic, and even slightly naive, belief that they had an almost mystical right to climb K2. "Our mountain of mountains" was how they put it. It was a disarming and disturbing view, far removed from our own rather pragmatic attitude towards the hills. The unspoken topic was our own intentions on the mountain. I found it quite embarrassing to keep up the pretence that we were still hoping to go back on the North-West Ridge and didn't think it could fool anyone. But I could see some sense in Al's reasoning that a blatant declaration of our changed intentions could result in a ban. So, despite the increasing warmth between Kurt and Julie and ourselves, there was still an element of gamesmanship at work on both sides.

While the weather was still so bad it made sense to retrieve as much as possible from our North-West Ridge Advance Base and Camp 1. Bev and I had already done a carry but after Renato's death I just couldn't summon the courage to go up the glacier again. The others did various carries and bit by bit most of the expensive items (including film equipment) came down. Future plans by now were very uncertain, for with each day that passed the chances of John and Aid making a last attempt on the Abruzzi receded.

Al, I felt, was beginning to clutch at straws and could see everyone leaving. Of the expeditions remaining, the Poles seemed to be the only ones that might possibly offer him some chance of staying on. In particular Dobroslawa Miodowicz-Wolf seemed keen to climb on the Abruzzi. Small and tough, and nicknamed "Mrufka" (Ant) because of her constant hard work, both on climbs and at Base Camp, she was disillusioned with the South-South-West Ridge. The deaths of the Americans and Casarotto had played their part but she also felt that the route was too hard for her. An attempt on the Abruzzi would stand a far higher chance of success. Mrufka had come very close to climbing Nanga Parbat in 1985 and had also been high on Broad Peak in 1984.

Her English was minimal and it was partly this that led to an unfortunate confusion. Al suggested that if the Polish South-South-West Ridge expedition failed and everyone from the British team went home, they might team up for a last attempt on the Abruzzi. Mrufka agreed with alacrity, but seemed to think that Al meant to start straight away.

"No, no," Al insisted. "You must climb with your friends on *your* route. Afterwards, if my friends go home, we will climb together on the Abruzzi." It was obvious that he was having trouble making himself understood and, in the end, seemed to have left the decision open, possibly unaware of how much Dave wanted to stay for one more effort.

Dave, as always somewhat taciturn, might have done better to formalise his intentions earlier with Al, who almost certainly hadn't given much thought to what was going to happen when the porters arrived. For by now it was clear that only a complete change in the weather, which seemed most unlikely, would stop Aid, John and Bev from going, and the porters would be here within the next two or three days. It was far from clear just who would be staying. I was looking for any excuse to go, and at one point even Al seemed prepared to admit defeat.

A pleasant and unexpected diversion from all this confused disillusionment arrived at Base Camp in the shape of a team of young climbers led by Andy Fanshawe. They had walked up from their own Base Camp on the Vigne Glacier, and on their first Himalayan expedition were attempting the complete traverse of Chogolisa which had never been done. They had only just arrived and had walked up as a training exercise, as well as to socialise and scrounge any spare food going. We were all impressed at their youthful exuberance and obvious unity of purpose. Andy had just been appointed National Officer of the British Mountain-eering Council, of which august body Al was Vice-President. "I appear to be your new boss," Al had quipped on being told the news of Andy's new job. They brought bits of gossip from Britain and were good company. We gave them a huge meal and the dubious privilege of sleeping in the big frame tent on its by now disgustingly dirty and uneven floor. Next morning they left, still in high spirits. We wished them well and hoped that their undertaking would not prove too ambitious on their first visit, for the whole traverse of Chogolisa looked a long and totally committing route, even if technically easy.

I think that in their presence we could all remember ourselves as young men and we made rueful comments about becoming senile old farts. Weeks later, back in the UK, we heard of their success: all of them completed the traverse of Chogolisa and then, minus Andy Fanshawe, they had attempted Broad Peak. On the col before the summit ridge Liam Eliot was killed when he fell through a cornice. Yet another tragedy.

The news that Al was contemplating climbing the Abruzzi with Mrufka hit Dave hard. He obviously felt let down by Al, who had, I felt, been manoeuvred to some extent into a position where whatever he did would be wrong. But Al had always found it desperately difficult to admit his mistakes and predictably tried to justify himself, which incensed Dave still further. Al, seemingly as a last resort, proposed a threesome which Dave rejected outright, pointing out that logistically everyone would get the worst of both worlds. As if to emphasise his decision Dave shaved off his beard to illustrate that his departure was imminent.

I was hopelessly torn between wanting to go home and a mixture of loyalties and unfulfilled ambitions that necessitated my staying on. To go would mean almost certainly no film and, if Al *did* climb K2, no ITN news reports either. Al and I had from the very earliest been involved in K2 together and I felt I owed it to him and also to Fullers to stay. In the end I admitted to myself that there was just no way I could leave Al on his own. But it was with a heavy heart that I told him and the others that I would stay on at Base Camp until it was resolved one way or the other. I felt as if I had lost my remission for good conduct and, while everyone else was being released, I would have to serve my full sentence.

The last day before the porters arrived

was spent packing. Al and I had decided to keep the absolute minimum of equipment.

"If I get up K2 I'll sell all my gear or just leave it on the mountain, it doesn't matter that much."

I packed everything except a very basic film kit and enough clothes to keep warm and walk out in. All my climbing gear went, as did all the exposed film. Slowly we assembled loads for the thirty or so porters we hoped would appear on the 28th to set off on the return march to Dasso.

Gloomily, I watched Aid, John, Dave and Bev prepare to depart. Al and I were going to move our meagre possessions over to the Strip after the others had gone. In dribs and drabs the porters arrived and loads were allocated and argued over. Remnants and rubbish were eagerly examined and fought over before being consigned to a bonfire. A constant eye needed to be kept on what was to stay, otherwise that too would have disappeared. I was worried about entrusting the exposed film to the others, not that I thought for one moment that they wouldn't guard it with their lives, I just found it hard to relinquish responsibility for its safety. But there was no choice if Al and I were to walk out quickly. Whatever happened, we aimed to be back in Islamabad with the hope of flying home on or around 20th August at the very latest. It might be much sooner, as there was no question of any more than one final attempt, and if that failed we might only be a few days behind the others.

As the day dragged on the stacks of loads diminished and small groups of porters left. Dave went with one group to try and get some more porters from Broad Peak Base Camp where, we understood, an expedition had recently arrived. The others left singly and somehow it seemed appropriate. There were no formal goodbyes and it seemed that the expedition was just petering out. At last the three or four porters we needed to take the remaining loads arrived and picked them up. Aid had gone without me being aware of it, which was sad, for I had got on well with him and wanted to say goodbye. John was the last to leave. After all their differences I was glad he and Al managed to depart on reasonably good terms.

Now the chips were down. Was there just a glimmer of hope that Al could salvage something from the wreckage? Or would we, too, follow the others back to Britain empty-handed?

Part Two

The Vigil

1

THROUGH the flickering heat of the bonfire, the last porter wavered out of sight down the moraine and out onto the Godwin Austen Glacier, to get to Concordia before nightfall. Al and I gleefully fed the flames with paraffin.

"I feel like the headmaster at the end of term after all the kids have gone," I remarked.

Al dubiously eyed my sooty face and hands: "You look more like the caretaker."

To my surprise I felt an unexpected surge of optimism. Al seemed to feel the same, and almost immediately the tensions of the last weeks ebbed away. The wide self-deprecating grin returned and Al became his boyish self once more, bubbling with enthusiasm and confidence. He talked of plans for the future: a possible joint expedition with Janusz Majer to Makalu, of rock climbing in America, and visits to Poland. My sister-in-law is Polish, living in London with relatives in Warsaw. I had long wanted to go to the Tatra mountains and Al was keen on rock climbing the weird and wonderful sandstone pinnacles of Northern Bohemia in Czechoslovakia. A joint venture seemed a good idea, with the Czechoslovakian Mountain Film Festival thrown in as well.

Occupied with clearing the site and making rambling plans for the future, late afternoon turned to early evening and we assembled heavy loads to carry over to the Strip to set up home again. We would have to return tomorrow to finish. As I gingerly lifted my sack, and buckled under its weight, I looked down to Concordia.

"Al, I don't want to seem too optimistic, but have you noticed something different?" Beyond Chogolisa the bank of cloud that had been present for the last weeks, whatever the weather, had disappeared. Now a strip of pale yellow evening sky shone clear and bright. "This could be it, you know."

"I've been thinking that myself. What's more, the barometer's going up."

We arrived on the Strip just in time to get my blue Snowdon Mouldings Limpet tent up before dark. Pitched in front of the Polish tents, it was, with so many expeditions departed, the last tent on the Strip. In front was an uninterrupted view of K2 with the huge diagonal line of the Abruzzi Ridge sweeping down from left to right.

It was strange suddenly being, in effect, on another expedition. Al and I stumbled into the Poles' big frame tent. We had been in often enough before, but now I felt slightly awkward, outnumbered by the six Poles and the Czechoslovakian, Peter Bozik. They all, nevertheless, made us welcome and we soon felt at ease. They had vast supplies of excellent meats: hams, dried beef and salamis of all shapes and sizes. They explained that it was only possible to get this quantity and quality of food on an expedition. In Poland most of the good quality food is exported. I wondered how far their higher standard of expedition living contributed to the Poles' astonishing successes on Himalayan expeditions in the last ten years!

The main Polish team were planning to leave again for the South-South-West Ridge the following evening and Al and

Mrufka would set off for the Abruzzi at the same time. When they had all gone I had thought I would make a two- or three-day sortie down to Concordia, and possibly further afield, to try to fill in some of the gaps in the film that the bad weather on the walk-in had caused. I had half arranged to visit the Chogolisa Base Camp, for I badly needed a long shot of K2 where the effects of foreshortening would be minimised. We had all got spectacular views of Chogolisa from our Base Camp and presumed the reverse view of K2 would be as good.

But, rather to my surprise, Janusz asked me if I would stay to act as Base Camp Manager, and, more important, maintain radio contact each evening with their team on the South-South-West Ridge. Weather forecasts each evening could be picked up from Radio Pakistan. We also arranged to open up the radio at eight each morning in case any message was necessary. Their Liaison Officer, who had previously done the job, had been summoned back to Islamabad due to the sudden illness of his father. I was pleased to be able to make myself useful but realised that time would hang heavy on my hands as there was nowhere interesting I could get to and back from between the morning and evening schedules.

While Janusz showed me how to change the battery packs, use the extension aerials, and so on, Al and Mrufka started planning for their climb. "Four days up and two down," Al announced. As they talked I became aware of an undercurrent of tension in the air and, when Al went out to our tent to collect something, I noticed that the two girls, Anna and Krystyna, were talking insistently to Mrufka who was on the verge of tears. She normally smiled constantly, her piercing blue eyes twinkling in amusement at our attempts to communicate with her, but now she seemed troubled. When Al returned I muttered to him that there appeared to be some sort of problem, and Janusz explained what was bothering everyone. This was simply that if Al and Mrufka were asked to pay another peak fee for attempting a different route, they, the Poles, simply couldn't afford it. Relieved that the problem was no bigger, Al reassured Janusz that he would take full

215

responsibility for any extra fee, pointing out that through his lectures, writing and the film it would be far easier for him as a Western climber to pay the fee than the Poles, who were already on an extremely tight budget.

The conversation gave Al an excuse to put forward an alternative plan he had been vaguely toying with, which was to join the Poles on the South-South-West Ridge. Al had not really wanted to give up on the North-West Ridge, though he had little choice in the matter, and he still saw an ascent of the Abruzzi as something of a consolation prize. If there was any possibility of being involved in a new route on K2, Al would still have preferred it. He pointed out that if he and Mrufka reverted to the South-South-West Ridge the Poles would be an eight, not a six-man team. But he was not taken up on his offer. At the time I thought that Janusz might not have understood Al, or possibly that he was worried that Al with his access to Western media would get more credit if they succeeded than he deserved. Mrufka, who had presumably decided not to go on the route anyway, must also have been relieved to stick to the Abruzzi. After all this had been sorted out, the air was cleared and we went to bed.

I had been sleeping very badly for the last week, suffering once more from the alarming but quite harmless Cheyne Stokes breathing. This is the phenomenon associated with altitude (and dying!) where shallow breaths are taken until breathing almost stops, then a great gulp of air exhaled. Breathing returns to normal and then the cycle repeats. It is alarming to listen to in other people and intensely irritating for the victim, who normally remains half asleep (or half awake) while it is happening, trying desperately to remember to breathe deeply, and as he drops off to sleep, promptly forgetting. I had had this on my arrival at Base Camp but it had soon stopped. Now it had come back. Was it a bad sign? We had now been at or above Base Camp for sixty-seven days. I was generally feeling much less fit than I had done a month before. John Barry had said that when he, Al and Dave Wilkinson had gone up to the old Camp 1 to retrieve gear a few days before he had felt desperately run down and thought Al was also very jaded.

Perhaps we had been here too long? Though I always understood that our present height of 5500 metres was still low enough to acclimatise fully, I had my doubts whether living at K2 Base Camp for so long was a good thing. From K2 it was hard to lose height quickly and in any case there is nowhere pleasant enough to want to go to recuperate. Living permanently on a glacier, even on the moraine, is a strain and it is impossible to unwind completely. The noise of avalanches, wind, falling stones, glacier movements, all provide background stress as well as straightforward physical discomfort. Even going to the loo at our old Base Camp could involve unpleasant slips on unstable boulders. Perhaps the cumulative effects were now making themselves felt.

In the morning Al and I returned to continue clearing up the mess, making an even bigger and better fire than the day before. On our own, I asked Al how he really felt. His reply was not totally reassuring.

"I think I'm still fine but, if I'm not,

I'll know it very quickly—probably by Advance Base and certainly by Camp 1. If it's no good we'll jack it in straight away and try and catch the others up." This last bit was pure Al optimism. By then they would have had at the very least a three-day start on a six- or seven-day walk. But as he spoke I wondered, looking down the glacier, now the weather signs were unmistakably good, would Aid perhaps return for one last fling? Unlikely. Once heading for home it is almost impossible to reverse the decision. Al had faced the same situation in 1983. He had waited three weeks, after his ascent of Broad Peak and the death of Pete Thexton, to attempt K2. When he eventually gave up and left, he had walked to Concordia in perfect weather and looked back at K2 with not a cloud in the sky. He had been sorely tempted to go back but knew in his heart of hearts that once on his way home, he couldn't psych himself up to return. He had walked out in an agony of self-doubt —had he missed his chance? It was obvious that the memory of 1983 was a strong influence in keeping Al here now.

"I've spent over four months of my life

at bloody K2 Base Camp, and I don't want to have to come back again."

The prospect of imminent fatherhood was also giving Al some cause for thought. Any mention of nappy-changing or baby food would guarantee a look of horror. As Al Burgess had once pointed out, Al was never very good at dealing with the past or the future, but was at his best coping with the immediacy of day to day decisions. So I had no doubt that he would be a convert when reality hit him, and I resolved to give him a few tips on the walk-out. He reckoned that, with the baby due at the end of August, he would still get home in time for the birth.

By now the fire was dying down, the cook tent had been dismantled and the rotting mounds of rubbish and dirt that littered its interior had been burned or chucked down a steep slope into a crevasse where we hoped it would never be seen again. I wondered how even our hardened stomachs had become immune to the bugs it must have contained. We were both wary about moving to the Strip, for we had had practically no stomach ailments since we arrived. Inevitably, we would now have a change of diet and water supply and the Strip was, if anything, even more squalid, with mini-mountains of old tins and containers scattered around. However carefully expeditions disposed of their rubbish, foraging porters would invariably find it and pick over the remains.

We carried rucksacks back to the Strip, clanking with tins of meat and fish to give to the Poles, who we knew would probably loathe them, but at least it showed we were making a gesture. Much earlier in the trip a petite and extremely beautiful young doctor from the Italian expedition had visited our Base Camp. Jim Hargreaves had tried to arrange a swap of food to vary our diets. She had taken one disdainful look at our boxes of tinned stew and asked us if we kept dogs! We also took some "hill food" for the attempt on the Abruzzi.

All through the afternoon Al and Mrufka prepared to leave in the evening. They planned to go up to Advance Base at night, sleep for an hour or so, then press on to Camp 1 before the sun hit the ridge. It was the usual scene of packing, re-packing, adding and discarding bits and pieces. Al eyed the food pile that Mrufka was assembling with mock horror.

"We're not going for a fortnight, you know," he explained patiently, as if dealing with a five-year-old. He removed most of the food, some of which Mrufka surreptitiously replaced, giving me a conspiratorial smile and a wink. He checked their joint climbing gear, for the Poles seemed to have fairly primitive equipment and clothing, lending Mrufka bits and pieces of his own. Mrufka prepared to pack a large figure-of-eight descendeur but Al dissuaded her, pointing out that a Sticht plate, normally used for belaying, was far lighter and could also be used for abseiling.

Later that day Al and Janusz went for a short walk up the Strip. Janusz seemed to be lecturing Al and was forcibly putting his points across. Al was nodding agreement and I got the impression that he was trying to warn Al not to over-estimate Mrufka's speed and strength. It seemed a good point, for Al always assumed that everyone was as fast as himself and found it very hard to understand that others might simply not be capable of keeping up with him.

The girls prepared an enormous evening meal, and at dusk everyone assembled, slightly tense, and charged with pent-up determination. Wojciech came in wearing a set of ludicrous woollen long johns that seemed to be endlessly stretchable and about five sizes too big. He did a good impersonation of Charlie Chaplin and broke the atmosphere; the meal proceeded with much banter and backchat from everyone. Both teams were planning on a four- or five-day ascent and there was a possibility of meeting on the summit. It was assumed that the South-South-West Ridge team would descend the Abruzzi, if they were successful, as Pietrowski and Kukuczka had done. We remembered to synchronise watches for the radio call, using my tried and trusted Seiko as the one most likely to tell the correct time. Then everyone returned to their tents and Al and Mrufka got ready to leave.

At the last minute Al asked if I fancied coming with them, at least as far as Advance Base, and possibly up to Camp 1 to film. I was sorely tempted, but we had already decided it would be politically unwise to be seen filming on the Abruzzi, and in any case I had sent all my hill gear, plastic boots, jumars, axes etc., back with the porters. Al had forgotten this, and the idea was dropped. But I wished we'd thought of it earlier.

We stood chatting in the dark waiting for Mrufka to come over from her tent. Al seemed very keyed up. Suddenly, out of the blue he told me he had a premonition that he wouldn't be coming back. I dismissed this by saying I had one every time I went climbing; so far it had been one hundred per cent wrong, and we changed the subject. Then Mrufka arrived and they prepared to leave.

"Well, we'd best get off. I can see this being a complete farce. Leaving at this time, we'll probably get hopelessly lost on the glacier and end up spending all night blundering around trying to find Advance Base. Okay. Well—um. See you in a few days then, Jim."

"Cheers, Al, good luck and take care."

Mrufka gave me a shy and rather unexpected embrace and the kiss-on-each-cheek that most Englishmen can never master. Then they set off.

The Poles were leaving for the South-South-West Ridge at around midnight and there seemed little point in staying up, so I wished them good luck, before going back to my tent. Ahead, Al and Mrufka's headtorches cast small pools of light, bobbing and dancing as they advanced to the end of the Strip. I paused for a few minutes outside my tent wishing them well.

2

THE morning of 30th July dawned fine and clear, though puffy clouds quickly built up around K2, but they seemed harmless. Unlike many recent nights it had been bitterly cold—a good sign, I thought, as I cracked the ice off the big water carrier outside the Polish Base Camp tents and made a brew. Now I was on my own I realised that I was the only English-speaking person left at Base Camp, except for the Liaison Officers attached to the remaining Koreans and Austrians. I spent a lot of the day bringing my tape diaries up to date. My Sony Professional Walkman quickly became my confidante. Not that there was anything new to report. Al and Mrufka hadn't returned, so presumably all was well. At six that evening Janusz opened up on the radio from their camp on the Negrotto Col. Already Wojciech, Peter and Przemyslaw had forged ahead and climbed straight to Camp 2, while Janusz and the two girls were camped on the Negrotto Col. Thus a day's gap was separating them and would be maintained. It made sense, for six people climbing together was both cumbersome and would cause over-crowding problems at cramped bivouac sites.

Kurt and Julie had left for the Abruzzi the day before, whether to film or to climb was unclear, but it didn't take much imagination to guess that, with the weather at last showing signs of settling down, they would be going for the top. The Koreans, too, were present in force on the mountain. They had been plugging away since their arrival in mid-June, and were without doubt highly organised, methodical and well-equipped. It was hard on them that, because of this, they were to some extent being used by other expeditions. With more than one permission on the same route, it was inevitable that expeditions would either have to join forces or at least co-operate with each other. But it would be fraught with problems of communication, logistics, duplication and language. The Austrian team was also on the Abruzzi, though I knew little about their numbers or movements.

The concept of the international expedition that Norman Dyhrenfurth had held so dear on Everest in 1971 now seemed to be happening by accident on K2. Would so many people moving up and down the mountain work out for good or bad? If harmony and co-operation prevailed, there could be a formidable collection of strong climbers breaking and maintaining trail which, after the bad weather, would be a more than normally arduous business higher up. But rivalry and discord could create a modern day Tower of Babel and the whole random collection of men and women striving for K2's summit might defeat themselves without any help at all from the mountain. It was an intriguing situation but one which, from the comfort and safety of Base Camp, I could only watch, and wait for an outcome.

There had been snow showers in the night, falling on the upper half of the mountain and blowing around the Abruzzi Ridge, but Thursday, 31st July was another reasonable day of blue skies and fluffy unthreatening clouds. I spent most of it filming sérac formation, icicles and reflections in glacier pools, "pretties" that could be slotted into a film to break up the action, and keeping a low profile at the other Base Camps, for I still felt slightly uneasy about Al being on the Abruzzi.

That conditions up there were not perfect was confirmed by the disgruntled arrival of two of the Austrian team carrying heavy loads and looking tired. As they passed my tent they stopped briefly: "No good—for us K2 is finished." They must have been on the mountain before the weather changed, and exhausted themselves. How frustrating, I thought, not only descending in improving weather but passing climbers still fresh on their way up. But I was still not convinced that Al and Mrufka's attempt would be any more than a last gesture of defiance. All the same I spent the day mentally urging those two little figures, whom I couldn't even see, up that colossal ridge, a 45° slope of rock, snow and ice, just winging up for ever. Looking out of the tent it was hard to believe the summit was over 3000 metres above my head. K2 is so huge that the previous day, walking towards the foot of the Abruzzi for about an hour and a half, the ridge didn't appear to have got any nearer at all. The scale of this mountain was still, after ten weeks, absolutely bewilderingly magnificent.

Next morning I waxed almost lyrical into the tape recorder:

Today is Friday, 1st August and it is a most beautiful and stunningly clear day. Last night I was awakened in the night with gusts of wind rattling the tent and my heart sank; this morning, there's a slight breeze, but the whole of K2 is in sunshine. The weather has really picked up, this is becoming one of the three spells of good weather we've had in the whole season—it is genuinely good weather. If the accumulation of snow at the top of the Abruzzi hasn't become too deep for trail-breaking, and there certainly will have been a lot of new snow up there, the next couple of days might well see a first British ascent of K2. For the first time, I'm now feeling a slight, and rather worrying, degree of optimism that they might actually pull it off at the last minute. The next two days will be absolutely critical. Al is intending to get to the top tomorrow. He can be a day late, perhaps. I suppose, if he's going incredibly well, he could be a day early, but once above 8000 metres, your survival-span is dramatically threatened, and he just cannot spend more than a couple of nights above 8000 metres without risking severe physical deterioration.

I think Al really deserves these three days of good weather. If he gets up K2 everything he's worked for and waited for and planned for will have come to fruition, and by waiting, by sticking it out, Al's shown himself to be the only person on the trip who's had the willpower and the commitment, and in that sense I think he richly deserves it. I just hope and pray that the weather holds and that Al does in fact do it.

Now that Al and Mrufka were well on their way, with nobody seeming to object, I could relax and start visiting the other camps. The Koreans, as usual, were inscrutably polite and friendly. Before he left Al had presented them with one of the two bottles of champagne that Jim Hargreaves had purchased from the British Club in Islamabad. We had kept them to celebrate in the event of our future success. Al had given one to the Koreans as a gesture of friendship but also, I suspect, by way of an apology for going on to the Abruzzi without telling them.

Now, sitting in their Base Camp tent, Kim Byong Joon, their leader, explained their plans. Three of them were moving up to Camp 4 for an oxygen-assisted summit bid. Five of the team had been turned back on 16th July (the day of Casarotto's accident) and since then most of the team had, like us, been waiting at Base Camp. But with more manpower available they had always kept Advance Base, and sometimes even Camps 1 and 2 manned, so that they could instantly take any advantage of good weather. Kim seemed amused at Al and Mrufka's presence on the Abruzzi and gently chided me with one of Al's stated excuses of "reconnaissance and photography", to my slight embarrassment. If Al and Mrufka had any sense they would be following in the footsteps of the

Koreans, but I could not get any clue as to their progress from Kim's radio contact with his team.

I returned to the empty Polish tent, by now feeling both reassured by the friendliness of the Koreans and buoyed up with optimism. I found myself thinking about the film: if Al got some good footage on Super 8 to go with what he, John Barry and Aid Burgess had already shot, I might be back in business. The twins had filmed on their abortive attempt on the Abruzzi and Aid said he thought he had quite good footage of House's Chimney. I went to sleep reliving the film I had shot in the last weeks and, despite knowing that there were still glaring omissions, thought that there was a chance of going home with a worthwhile story after all.

I awoke early next morning and quickly checked the weather, then, as was becoming a habit, recorded my thoughts on tape.

Today is Saturday, 2nd August and should be the day that Al and Mrufka get to the summit. Quite frankly I'm gripped rigid sitting down here on my own at Base Camp. I woke up this morning to another fine day, but what appears to be heat haze is making Chogolisa down the valley look fainter. There is cloud coming up from the south-east, which as far as I know we haven't had before. K2 itself is clear, there're some white clouds hanging around the middle of the Abruzzi. It's a perfect summit day if Al is on schedule. If he's not, and it's going to take another day, I very much fear that the weather may be deteriorating and by tomorrow be bad again.

In that case we'll have a situation very similar to Maurice and Liliane, and also to Kurt and Julie who only just got away with it on their attempt and subsequent descent in storm. The crucial thing with the Abruzzi is to get to the summit and then as quickly as possible down to the top of the fixed ropes, which are at about 7300 metres. Then, really, you're laughing. It's just a question of abseiling down interminably. Unless you make a daft mistake with the descendeur, or a rope breaks, the trip's virtually over. It's just endurance, plodding down hill, putting one foot in front of another back down to Base Camp. But the top of the Abruzzi in bad weather is a death trap and, as Michel Parmentier nearly found out, it's a desperately difficult place to escape from.

... Down from the Shoulder to the sérac barrier is featureless, very avalanche-prone, you have to hit the sérac barrier at exactly the right spot, and really the top section of the Abruzzi is an extraordinarily difficult place to extricate yourself from if you can't see where you're going. The summit ridge is technically not very difficult, but there is one section of steep ice, an ice traverse, before the summit ridge itself is gained. If they're there today they should in theory be up and down while the weather stays good. It's obviously not going to crack up in the next hour or so. I'd be very surprised if it did, but I think by this evening, if the usual pattern is followed, there will be some cloud coming in and the weather deteriorating, a haze round the summit, and by tomorrow stormy conditions will be back again, so I'm hoping and praying now that today is Al's summit day and that he's well on his way there, and by this evening, if he follows his declared schedule, he should be well down the mountain by the end of the evening.

The previous evening's radio call to the Polish team had been very encouraging. Wojciech, Peter and Przemyslaw were bivouacking at 8000 metres and Janusz, Anna and Krystyna were now at Camp 3. The two groups had since lost radio contact with each other, either through dead ground intervening or, as I had no response from them either, because the leading climbers had still been engrossed in the climbing or had been preparing a bivouac site. With any luck they would now top out before the end of the day; they knew that the last section of the South-South-West Ridge was not technically very difficult. It had been climbed in 1981 by the successful Japanese West Ridge Expedition, who had made a long rightwards traverse across snowfields to reach the ridge only a couple of hundred metres below the top. The Hunza climber,

Nazir Sabir, who had climbed the route with the Japanese and now ran a trekking agency in Islamabad, had described this last section as being quite straightforward. Janusz and the girls would take another day but presumably would reach the top on the third.

There was no news of Kurt and Julie, nor the remaining Austrians. Four of them were now back in Base Camp, which left three somewhere on the Abruzzi around Camps 3 or 4.

Later the same morning I went to visit the Koreans and received a nasty surprise. They thought Al had given up his summit attempt and spent last night at Camp 2. He should have been spending the night at Camp 4, so must therefore be on his way down. It looked as if the 1986 Fullers British K2 Expedition had finally ground to a halt.

I took a couple of flasks of lemonade and some food and set off, walking for about half an hour until I could see the short icefall that guarded the way to Advance Base. There I settled down on a flat rock, watching the points where any descending figures should be visible, but I could see nobody. If Al and Mrufka were on their way down from Camp 2 they should be back in Base Camp by late morning, unless there had been some sort of mishap. At around 3.30 p.m. I gave up and returned, puzzled, to Base Camp.

The previous day the same Korean had told me that four climbers had been avalanched from the summit of Gasherbrum IV and fallen down the West Face. This had seemed a very unlikely story and none of the porters or either of the Liaison Officers had heard anything about it. Had I misunderstood? Or had the Koreans got it all wrong? Was it even a practical joke demonstrating some weird Oriental sense of humour? I just didn't know, but as every minute passed it seemed less and less likely that Al and Mrufka were coming down, and I allowed my spirits to rise a couple of points.

At six I called up Janusz again. The reception was not as good as it had been and Janusz also sounded very breathless. Krystyna with her higher pitched voice took over, which was far easier to understand. I gathered that they had made contact with Wojciech at eight that morning and he had said that he, Przemyslaw and Peter hoped to go to the summit that day. Neither I nor the Koreans had any news of this happening, and once again I could get no response from my call. Now Janusz and the girls were at Casarotto's last bivouac site at around 8100 metres. Above them Wojciech must either be on the summit or not far below it. We arranged another call at eight and signed off.

At the bottom of the Strip a party of trekkers had arrived. To my delight they were Americans and I bounded down to talk to them. In my pleasure at speaking English once more without communication problems, I babbled on for over an hour. I think they must have been quite amused. They had had a perfect walk-in and the following day were going back to Concordia, then onto the Gasherbrum Glacier. They would be back at Concordia on the night of the 7th and starting their walk back to Dasso on the 8th. With any luck they would have a couple of spare porters available by then and I made a very open-ended arrangement to meet them and go back together. Pleased with the way things seemed to be working out, I tried, once more unsuccessfully, to contact Wojciech and wended my way back to my tent.

As I passed the Korean tent I was told that Al and Mrufka were now at Camp 4, along with Kurt, Julie and three Koreans, all of whom would be going for the top in the morning! It seemed amazing that, since the first attempt on K2 by Eckenstein and Crowley in 1902, it still hadn't had a British ascent, but now, eighty-four years later, there was a good chance of it being climbed by two Britons on two different expeditions on the same day. All the same I couldn't help a slight chill of apprehension sweeping over me, although there was no obvious reason for it.

I awoke early on 3rd August, and paced restlessly backwards and forwards the 100 metres between my tent and the Koreans', seizing on any new information. I could feel my face muscles ache with the strain. The account of the day on my tape diary shows how the events unravelled.

Today is Sunday, 3rd August, and as

far as the British K2 expedition is concerned, today is the day. Al and Mrufka apparently spent the night camped next to the Korean tent at 7900 metres, which gives them just over 700 metres to climb. The tension is absolutely unbearable. It's ten o'clock. The weather is certainly not good. It's beginning to deteriorate. There's high cloud moving in. The summit appears and disappears, there's cloud round it, and it's much windier than it was yesterday. I think the weather will remain okay for today but I don't hold out much hope for tomorrow.

There are quite a few people up there: the Koreans, Al and Mrufka, Kurt and Julie, presumably the Austrians and also, of course, the Poles coming up the South-South-West Ridge who should top out today. Three of them may well have done that yesterday. This could be a big bonus if they did, because there'll be a trail coming down from the top, which could make life a lot easier. But I haven't heard anything from Wojciech and his team and don't know what their position is. The radio contact with the

Koreans seems to be almost continuous but as they studiously give me information that transpires to be completely wrong about half an hour later, it's almost easier for me not to know what's going on and sit outside my tent fretting. Whatever happens there's nothing I can do about it anyway and whatever will happen will happen, and I'll find out sooner or later. So I am about as tense and gripped about the outcome as I've ever been and concerned for the welfare not just of Al but of all the climbers who are really on the borderlines up there. Most of them are without oxygen, and the next twenty-four hours should see the whole saga of K2 for 1986 resolved one way or the other.

. . . It's half past twelve, still on the 3rd, and still no news, but clouds are now beginning to well up all around; K2 summit's clear at the moment, but big puffs of cloud are drifting past, the wind's obviously getting up and Broad Peak has got a cloud cap covering its three summits completely, so the weather's definitely on the turn and I

Evening light on the West Face and summit of K2. The Mushroom is the large hanging glacier in the centre of the picture. *(Jim Curran)*

Przemyslaw Piasecki crosses the Mushroom. *(Janusz Majer)*

One of the cruxes of the South-South-West Ridge. *(Janusz Majer)*

Dave Wilkinson on the fixed ropes above Camp 2 on the first unsuccessful British attempt on the Abruzzi
(Al Rouse)

Aid Burgess on the ladder below House's Chimney. *(Al Burgess)*

The wreck of Camp 3 which greeted Piasecki and Bozik on 4th August. *(Peter Bozik)*

A rare clearance gives a view of the summit with the high winds still driving across it. *(Jim Curran)*

Above: Kurt Diemberger and Julie Tullis's tent at Advance Base. *(Jim Curran)*

Below: Ghulam, film porter impossible, mail runner and opportunist. *(Jim Curran)*

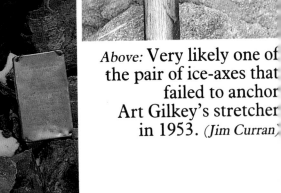

Above: Very likely one of the pair of ice-axes that failed to anchor Art Gilkey's stretcher in 1953. *(Jim Curran)*

Left: The Gilkey memorial, with later additions. *(Jim Curran)*

Watching and waiting at Base Camp, Michael Messner, the solitary Austrian (left), and Krystyna Palmowska of Poland. *(Jim Curran)*

Advance Base at the bottom of a storm-swept Abruzzi Ridge, but no-one in sight. *(Jim Curran)*

Four of five who died at or near Camp 4 during the storm:
above left/right, Al Rouse and his Polish partner, Mrufka
Wolf. *(Jim Curran).* Below left and right, the Austrians,
Alfred Imitzer and Hannes Wieser. *(Michael Messner)*

Distraught and exhausted survivors of Camp 4, (above)
Kurt Diemberger, and (below) Willi Bauer. *(Jim Curran)*

Farewell to the Baltoro, Mustagh Tower, above, and below, the North Ridge of Masherbrum. *(Jim Curran)*

think whatever's happening up there, it's now going to be a bit of a race against time.

. . . It's two o'clock. I've just made contact with Janusz on the bivouac that Casarotto and Wojciech used and he says the weather is very bad. What's ironic is, looking at the crest of the ridge only some hundred metres to his left, it's completely clear. So it must be very windy, but obviously within the cloud on the South-South-West Ridge there's quite a storm blowing. This also means of course that the Abruzzi will be getting it as well, which is very worrying. There's no news at all of Al, or the Koreans, or the Austrians, but I'll go down to the Korean tents and check that out.

. . . It's now half past two on Sunday, 3rd August and to say I'm worried is an understatement. The score so far as I can make out is this: Janusz and the two girls, Krystyna and Anna, are bivouacking at Casarotto's high point (8100 metres), and not moving at all today.

The weather's bad, it's blowing hard and it's cold, and survival up there is definitely finite. Unless the weather's perfect tomorrow, I think I must urge them to come down and come down quickly at my next contact.

Higher up, Wojciech and the two lads haven't been seen.

I had been quietly concerned about Janusz's team for the last two or three radio calls. He was beginning to sound unclear and disorientated and out of breath even at rest. Krystyna was more coherent, but perhaps the insidious effects of oxygen lack were beginning to show without them realising it. I remembered reading years ago in *Everest the Hard Way* an account of a radio call between Dr. Charlie Clarke and Chris Bonington where Charlie had told Chris that he was troubled by his increasing vagueness, and I wondered if I was witnessing the same sort of symptoms. Unlike Charlie, I was not a doctor, neither was I a member of the Polish expedition. I didn't imagine that they'd take kindly to any suggestion on my part that it would be wiser to retreat. But I felt that somehow

I had to at least voice my doubts and let them make the decision themselves.

There was nothing to be done just yet and I strolled down to visit the Koreans again:

I've just been across to the Korean camp and expressed my concern. I haven't made radio contact with Wojciech for two days and as far as I know nobody else has either, although this may be wrong. I find the language problem with the Koreans so difficult, it's very hard to tell what's happening. The Koreans say their three have reached the last sérac and are within two hours of the top. Because they're using oxygen, they are breaking trail and obviously everyone else will want to follow them. Now because of the cloud, they don't know, or can't see, whether anyone else *is* following them or not, and again the message is confusing. Whether Kurt and Julie and Al and Mrufka and Uncle Tom Cobleigh and all are somewhere behind them, I just don't know. Everyone, apart from the Koreans, seems to have a big question mark hanging over them and the team I'm really concerned about now is the lead Polish three, Wojciech and co. I just hope and pray they're all right. They should have reached the summit yesterday and apparently didn't. Or if they did, they haven't got as far down the Abruzzi as the top camp or past the Koreans, which is very worrying.

. . . It's just past three o'clock. There's a lot of excitement down at the Korean camp. They've got a huge telephoto lens and binoculars and they're in constant radio contact with the Korean summit party, who are now very near the top.

At half past three the Koreans excitedly beckoned me over to look through their big telephoto lens and I heaved a sigh of relief:

Well, that's reassuring: I can actually see Wojciech and co through the Korean monster thousand-mm lens, climbing very near the summit, making slow progress, but I know they're on the final part of the ridge that Nazir Sabir says is

246

not that difficult. So hopefully they'll get to the top today. . . . If I could will Al up the last section of K2 I would. I feel desperately far away at the moment and only able to gaze helplessly through this big telephoto lens at this little silent charade that's going on ten or eleven thousand feet above my head.

By now, fretful and trying not to show it, I could hardly bear to speak to anyone. At 4.15 the Korean radio crackled into life and the camp erupted in joy. The summit! Kim, the leader, smiling broadly, was mobbed by everyone. A few Hunza high-altitude porters did an impromptu dance, and from nowhere the strangest cocktails I have ever seen were produced: whisky and mandarin oranges. Everyone drank a toast and some of us managed to grab a re-fill. But my heart wasn't in it and my congratulations were forced.

Despite the festivities, I urged Kim to ask the summiteers yet again if there were signs of anyone else. Frequently they opened up and, excited, breathless voices came over. The atmosphere was electric, but I couldn't understand a word. Then

Kim told me that the Koreans had still seen no-one and that they didn't think the others had followed them. Utterly deflated and worn out with the tension of the afternoon, I walked slowly back to my tent, brain whirling with unanswerable questions.

It's now a quarter past seven and I shall briefly try and sum up what has been a gruelling day. The Koreans are on their way down to Camp 4, their top camp, they're out of radio contact and so any news about Al, Kurt, Julie, etc. is non-existent. In fact there hasn't been any news about them all day. It's feasible they could walk into Base Camp in ten minutes' time, having set off down early this morning, but I don't think so. The Poles must be at or near the summit because we saw them this afternoon. They're about to face their third bivouac; at least, one, possibly two, more than they intended, so they must be desperately stretched and therein lies the makings of an epic.

I am having to do a Sherlock Holmes on the position of Kurt, Julie, Al and

Mrufka and the Austrians. It seems to me that all of them must have spent the day at Camp 4 and the wisdom of this is not clear. Al has often said you never spend more time than you have to around 8000 metres and Camp 4 is 7900. It's too high. Whether all of them are knackered, whether just one or two of them are, is pure speculation, but I would imagine that, if the weather does hold, and it's looking very dodgy indeed, although it did clear later on in the afternoon, they may possibly be thinking of a go at the top tomorrow. Obviously, as every hour passes, the chances of them getting there are slimmer and slimmer and my own feeling now is that they will, in fact, abandon the climb and start descending tomorrow—that's assuming they're all okay. That's only a guess and I suppose there is the slimmest of outside chances that they still might make it but, quite frankly, I very much doubt it now.

At seven a.m. on the 4th I awoke to hear my name being called insistently.

"Mr. Jim, Mr. Jim, I have some very

bad news." It was the Austrian Liaison Officer, Capt. Neer Khan.

Instantly awake with my heart pounding like a steam train, I hastily unzipped the tent door. Capt. Neer peered in, his dark eyes troubled behind a large pair of spectacles.

"I am afraid that one of the Poles is dead, poor fellow. He has perished in the night on his descent from the summit."

I nodded dumbly. "Do you know which one?"

"No, that we have not discovered."

He didn't have to tell me: a vision of Wojciech flashed in front of me, puffing at his stubby pipe, fooling around in his long johns. I knew it was him.

At eight a.m. I tried the radio and overheard the subdued Polish voices talking to each other. Janusz and the girls had at last managed to get contact with the two survivors, who must be in Camp 4. I couldn't understand what was being said, though I could guess, and couldn't tell who was speaking. I urgently wanted to interrupt, but felt it would be intrusive not to let them finish. Apart from wanting to know what had happened, I was desperate for news of all the others. I waited for a change of voice to indicate that the call was about to finish, then interrupted, but to my dismay both calls had finished at exactly the same moment and I got no response. I could have kicked myself for I instantly realised that I had missed the chance to suggest to the two survivors in Camp 4 that they leave their radio there for Al and Mrufka if, as I had heard from Capt. Neer, they had decided to go for the summit.

This last was only a rumour from the Koreans, and I found it hard to credit. Clouds were beginning to drift across the Shoulder but worse was a high feathery scurry of cloud racing in from the south. It was already over Chogolisa and was the clearest indication yet that the good weather spell was at an end. Surely, with yet another death and a storm brewing, everyone would now be coming down? Janusz and the girls, in particular, would be courting disaster if they didn't. With their rest day, they were now at least two days from the summit, even if they went at the same pace as the leading team, who had themselves been desperately slow.

Anxiously I went down to the Austrian Base Camp and we all took it in turns with a large pair of binoculars trained on the South-South-West Ridge. We could now see the Poles at the Casarotto Bivouac. At ten, to my relief, we spotted them, definitely moving downwards. One of the Austrians, called Michael Messner, spoke good English and told me, to my utter amazement, that there were three Austrians going for the summit who had already been at or above Camp 4 for three nights. I commented in near despair to my diary:

The sky is now getting greyer and greyer by the moment and it seems like everyone up there has got summit fever and is going for it despite the knowledge that the Barrards, the two Poles, Piotrowski and Kukuczka, and everyone else who's spent too long near the summit has met with disaster. One can only hope and pray that either they all have a collective fit of common sense and come down, or that they make it to the top and all get down safely. But it's getting very difficult to sustain much more emotion about this. It's getting almost out of hand, one's just left with a feeling of terrible flatness and anticlimax. Why do people seem to run against well tried and proven methods of climbing on the three big ones, Everest, K2 and Kanch, which extract such appalling death tolls? Over and over again people seem to make almost identical mistakes. It's sad, futile and tragic, and I just can't wait to get away from this place now. But from my privileged position at Base Camp it's very easy to be wise before, during and after the event.

By half past four the last of the weak and hazy sunshine had gone and the sky was completely overcast. Great grey scudding clouds had gathered round K2. At five swathes of snow were drifting across the whole of the South Face of K2 and Broad Peak. It wasn't snowing at Base Camp but it was only a matter of time. As six approached I prepared myself for radio contact with Janusz and final confirmation of who had been killed. Scarcely any doubt, for the Koreans had radioed from

Camp 4 it was "the man without a moustache", which could only be Wojciech. Just before I opened up more news arrived from the Koreans. One of their high-altitude porters had been killed by a falling stone between Advance Base and Camp 1. The eighth death, the second today, the nightmare continued.

At six I opened up to find Capt. Neer already talking. It *was* Wojciech. He had had some mishap with a fixed rope but details were vague. Przemyslaw and Peter, who had been to the summit with him, were descending from Camp 4 on the Abruzzi to Camp 3. Janusz and the girls were hoping to get down in two days. A long discussion followed with the Captain about how to prevent the news of Wojciech's death being leaked to the press before his relatives were told. The Captain sensibly said that the first priority was to get everyone down before any news was released and that they weren't to worry. I joined in the call, offering my condolences to Janusz and urging them to be careful and keep coming down. Krystyna broke in tearfully, "There have been too many deaths on the mountain this year." And at that heartfelt note we signed off.

In the Korean tent Kim, too, was on the verge of tears. Mohammed Ali, the Sirdar of the high-altitude porters, had been climbing between Advance Base and Camp 1 when he had been hit by a falling stone and killed outright. Radio calls were being made back and forth and the rest of the porters had decided they could bury Mohammed Ali almost where he lay under a moraine. Kim urged them to make sure that it was a safe and good enough place for a grave. Then in his halting English he explained that for the Korean expedition their motto had always been safety first—success second. For him, the death of Mohammed Ali had diminished the Koreans' achievements. Suddenly Kim looked very tired and old as the strain caught up with him. He was embarrassed at showing his emotions in front of me and I soon left.

I walked in the deepening murk and gloom, back up the Strip. Now the cloud was down on the glacier and it was raining, in that persistent nearly-sleet way that is common in Scotland. I brought my diary up to date and fell asleep almost immediately. Sleep was rapidly becoming an escape from reality.

I awoke with a start at 4.30 a.m. and cautiously unzipped the tent. Not quite pitch dark, no wind but silently and steadily three or four inches of snow had fallen. Groaning with dismay, I burrowed back into my sleeping bag and tried not to think too hard. Dozing intermittently I could hear the soft thump thud of new snow avalanches all around.

3

A T six I woke up properly. Stepping outside I realised that all the Polish tents were in dire need of attention. Four inches of heavy wet snow on the Base Camp tent needed pushing off from inside to avoid the frame buckling. Half an hour of cold and miserable stumbling around followed before I could put a stove on inside the big tent and sit trying to warm my hands. What it must be like on the Shoulder I couldn't, and didn't want to, imagine.

Krystyna came on the air at eight a.m. Once more, my tape diary for the day tells the story:

The weather's still pretty grim, it's starting to snow again. It's half past nine in the morning of 5th August and I've been in contact with Krystyna. She said that they're very worried about the two surviving Poles on the Abruzzi who are now at Camp 3. They should in theory be okay, they're on the fixed ropes, but apparently they were nearly dead when they arrived at Camp 4 yesterday morning after Wojciech's death and they're not out of the woods yet. There's still, of course, no news about the seven who tried for the summit yesterday.

. . . It's half past eleven now and there's a slight clearing around the Abruzzi—the lower third is out of cloud and there's a little bit of blue sky which is just enough to emphasise the high wind swirling round, blowing the cloud off in spirals. The top two-thirds are still deep in cloud which stretches away down the valley towards Chogolisa, black and threatening, and there's obviously more bad weather on the way.

. . . It's about half past one in the afternoon and the weather's now worse than it's ever been. It's blowing hard at Base Camp and lashing down with rain. I think if this carries on we're going to have to be prepared to expect the worst. There are actually twelve people on K2 at the moment, all at or above 7000 metres and the weather up there must be horrendous.

During the afternoon a group of figures appeared at the end of the Strip. It would be the successful Koreans and a team of high-altitude porters. I didn't really imagine it was anyone else, and forced myself not to be disappointed when, a few minutes later, I was proved correct. As they passed I muttered my congratulations to the Koreans, Kim Chang Sun, Jang Bong Wan and Jang Byong Ho, and condolences to the porters, who were very subdued. They, not surprisingly, had no news of the others. Kim later told me that they had left each camp with food, fuel and stoves for any descending climbers. They could throw no light on why the seven had not followed them to the summit on the 3rd and seemed as puzzled as I was. Al and Mrufka had now been on the mountain for six days, Kurt and Julie for seven. I didn't know how long the Austrians had been there, but they would have spent at least three nights above 8000 metres and had already made one unsuccessful attempt on the summit. Everyone had now been over 8000 metres for far too long.

As I could do nothing at the present except keep urging the Polish B team down the mountain, I kept my concern for the fate of the others at the back of my mind. At least being able to talk to Krystyna gave me the illusion that I was doing something and certainly she always seemed pleased to hear my voice. On each call I tried to be as positive as possible about the weather, saying (truthfully) that every hundred metres of height lost would improve their chances and (untruthfully) another thousand metres would bring them out of the cloud and virtually to the end of their troubles. I didn't really expect them to believe this but there was no point telling them what I really felt, which was that everyone on the mountain now would be lucky to get down alive.

With little else to do but worry, my fears for the others surfaced in my tape diary:

They don't actually form a terribly strong unit. Al's been at K2 Base Camp for seventy-three days, failed on the route he really wanted to do, has had to get revved up for the Abruzzi and, although he went well on the North-West Ridge, struck me as being somewhat frail, his drive and ambition maybe outstripping his physical prowess.

Kurt Diemberger, the old veteran, legend in his own lifetime, he's now in his mid-fifties and with the best will in the world, although he's as strong as an ox, he's a very slow, plodding, old-school climber and one wonders just how long he can keep going at his age without oxygen.

Julie is, I would have thought, the least experienced, though I can't speak for the Austrians. She's done some pretty remarkable things in the last few years and has come to big mountains late in life. This is her third trip to K2 and she's already climbed Broad Peak with Kurt. The problem with Julie is again ambition outweighing perhaps skill and physical ability. Although her determination is obviously not in doubt.

Mrufka, we don't know that well. She's got a determined reputation in the Polish team. How she'll be bearing up to this strain, with the added knowledge that Wojciech is dead, is hard to say.

As for the three Austrians, they have been up there three nights, have already tried for the top and failed, which means either conditions weren't good enough or, they weren't strong enough or possibly they weren't good enough. It has to be remembered that on their first attempt Kurt and Julie were turned back by technical difficulties on this last bit of steep ice which I think is probably where Wojciech fell off, although we'll have to wait to confirm that. So it does seem to me that it's a group of people with the rather appalling combination of extreme ambition but perhaps collectively not the physical push. They should certainly not be at or around 8000 metres on K2 in what by now must be a raging storm with no oxygen, and limited food and gas.

That evening the radio call with Krystyna revealed that the weather on the South-South-West Ridge was dreadful, and the wind was still ferocious. Krystyna continued to be terribly concerned about

Peter and Przemyslaw, but didn't enquire about Mrufka or any of the others. I reckoned she had enough to worry about, so avoided mentioning them myself. By now it was they who needed all the encouragement that was going. Peter and Przemyslaw were by now either relatively safe or dead.

More as a gesture than anything else, I tried to raise Camp 4 in the unlikely event that the Poles had left their radio there. No reply, but the hiss and crackle of static. A fine dusting of powder snow blew under the door of the big frame tent, and I turned off the radio and the Camping Gaz lamp and went to bed.

On the morning of 6th August I went for a walk up the Strip. I had been doing this regularly, partly to relieve the tension but also to get nearer the Abruzzi and see if I could spot anyone coming down. Janusz and the girls were still at least a day away from Base Camp, but there was some cause to hope that Peter Bozik and Przemyslaw Piasecki would get back today. No sign of them, but on my return Michael Messner of the Austrian team came up to talk to me. Michael was in his early twenties (no relation of Reinhold) and, I discovered to my surprise, the only member of the Austrian team still at Base Camp, the others already having left for home. He had the large pair of binoculars I had used earlier to spot the Poles on the Casarotto Bivouac and he told me now that he had picked out two figures descending the moraine below Advance Base at the foot of the Abruzzi.

Temporarily my spirits rose. At least two people were off the mountain. Michael reckoned they would be back in an hour or so. I put a large saucepan of water on the stove and we both set out to meet them.

At the end of the moraine, in the same place as I had waited for Al and Mrufka during the false alarm, we met Peter and Przemyslaw. Silent handshakes, muttered expressions of relief, commiseration and muted congratulations. We walked slowly back to the tents, and I filmed them coming in the last few yards. They disappeared to their own tents to drop their sacks and change into dry clothing before coming into the Base Camp tent. At last, their ordeal over, they silently shook hands with each other. No words were needed and none said. I handed them their cups.

Peter spoke no English, but Przemyslaw's, I was pleased to discover, was better than I had thought, and slowly he told me what had happened, as far as he knew.

The first mystery, the death of Wojciech, he could cast little light on. They had been descending utterly exhausted from the summit with the Koreans and, at the bottom of a section of fixed rope with a gap in it, Wojciech had failed to arrive. He had either collapsed or fallen; they weren't quite sure and were desperate to go down to the Korean Base Camp tents to find out any more details.

They had carried on down to Camp 4 where they had found Al and Mrufka and got into their tent. Al had moved outside to make room for them, and he and Mrufka had set off for the top at about half past five, followed by Kurt and Julie and two of the three Austrians. The other had stayed in Camp 4, presumably too tired to make a summit bid. They had left Camp 4 at around 10.30 a.m. (bringing the radio with them, as I had feared) and had seen the others well on their way through weather that was slowly worsening. Al, Przemyslaw was at pains to explain, was leading, not carrying a rucksack, and wearing his red one-piece down suit. It was a poignant image that I could, and still can, visualise quite easily. I wondered if he had taken the small Super 8 camera and reflected that it would be just like Al not to bother with it, to save that bit of extra weight.

Their descent had been gruelling but uneventful. Camp 3 was apparently half wrecked by an avalanche. They seemed in reasonable health, though Peter had frost-bitten toes and started bathing them in warm water.

Their arrival gave me limited cause for optimism, for they had started down at least a day earlier than the others would have done, and they said that it had not snowed quite so hard higher up the mountain. Perhaps I had been grossly over-pessimistic. After all, Janusz and the girls were now well on their way down. Why shouldn't everyone else be following? (Deep down I knew bloody well why, but at that moment I felt a need to celebrate a bit of good news.) Please God, I thought, let them all arrive tomorrow.

Later in the afternoon Przemyslaw and Peter and I went to visit the Koreans to try and sort out the events of the night of the 3rd-4th August. Two of the Korean summiteers were there with Mr. Kim, but the third, Kim Chang Sun, was apparently resting in his tent. The Korean Liaison Officer and Capt. Neer were also there. The discussion that followed was in English but unfortunately no-one spoke or understood it well enough to grasp any more than the simplest statements. Capt. Neer and I acted as interpreters in the widest sense of the word, and tried to make out what had occurred. What follows is my understanding of events from both sides but, due to the very real difficulties everyone had in communicating, it is still only an impression.

The three successful Koreans had left the summit at around 4.45 p.m. on 3rd August. As they descended they saw small lumps of snow bouncing past them and realised that the three Poles were behind and above. Without oxygen, which they had finished and left on the summit, two of the Koreans were moving very slowly. But Kim Chang Sun was the fittest and went on ahead. On the way up he had noticed a dangerous gap in the ramshackle collection of fixed ropes left by various expeditions that by now protected some or all of the awkward sections above the Bottleneck Couloir. He cut the end off one rope to bridge the missing section, but left the shortened end trailing, presumably reckoning that it was straightforward enough to climb down unprotected to the beginning of the next rope. He then carried on down to Camp 4.

Peter and Przemyslaw were next down and with headtorches safely negotiated the obstacle, one calling back to the other to warn him. Above them were Jang Bong Wan, Wojciech and Jang Byong Ho. Wojciech was moving very slowly, and behind him one of the Koreans was so exhausted he tied himself to a piton and decided to bivouac, slumped upright. In front of Wojciech the other Korean was told of the gap in the ropes. He climbed back past Wojciech to try (unsuccessfully) to persuade his companion to come down. At the bottom of the ropes Przemyslaw and Peter had waited an hour before just one Korean came down the ropes. There was no sign of Wojciech but earlier they had heard a noise which they thought might have been someone falling. The three had descended to Camp 4 and the remaining Korean had come down at first light. It seemed almost certain that Wojciech had unknowingly (he had no headtorch) abseiled off the end of the rope to his death.

Now back at Base Camp Przemyslaw, in particular, seemed to find this very hard to accept and in his fraught state (for he was obviously still extremely tired) seemed to think the Koreans at fault for not passing the message on successfully. I did my best to defuse the situation, for it seemed to me that everyone concerned had been in such a state of extreme exhaustion that rational decisions were a lot to expect.

An example of how totally shattered the Koreans were was provided by an extraordinary statement that they had passed Kurt and Julie at the bottom of the fixed ropes. This I thought couldn't possibly be correct. Eventually I gathered that when the second Korean met Peter and

Przemyslaw at the bottom of the ropes, he assumed in his daze of exhaustion that they were Kurt and Julie ascending! It was an indication of how oxygen lack and extreme fatigue can confuse understanding and these factors too would have contributed to the accident. The three Poles, without sleeping bags and having had two bivouacs already, must have arrived on the summit on their last legs. An accident on the descent was, like Petrowski's earlier, almost inevitable.

Though I didn't mention it, of course, the Poles should not have been relying on the Koreans' fixed ropes in the first place. But when the ropes were there and others were using them, it would be ridiculous to expect them to ignore them, either on purist or practical grounds. It could be said that the accident occurred as a result of an act of faith on the part of the Poles who perhaps too readily assumed that, once they reached the top, they would be safe on the Abruzzi. But there was no point in putting my oar in, and eventually the air was cleared more or less to everyone's satisfaction. It still seemed tragic and ironic, however, that Kim's actions in adjusting the ropes had done precisely what he had set out to prevent.

It was time for the evening call to Krystyna and I gave Przemyslaw the radio.

"You call her. It will be a nice surprise for them."

He found, to our relief, that they had managed to get down to the Negrotto Col and now only had the big couloir to descend to the Filippi Glacier where Casarotto had been killed. Their voices sounded, if not stronger, then a bit more cheerful. But the weather which had shown signs of a slight improvement, had deteriorated again, and as I went off to my tent it was snowing gently.

I awoke early as usual on the 7th, and still with a bit of optimism reported the first impressions of the day:

Once more it's snowed in the night. I've woken up to a wintry landscape, but the wind has dropped. K2 is clear up to the Shoulder and the pinnacle behind which Camp 4 lies is also visible, so the whole of the Abruzzi and the whole of the descent is out of cloud. It's hard to tell how much wind is up there but it's certainly not as windy as last night and anyone up there will, I imagine, be hot-footing it down. The big question is, *is* there anyone up there? I think the euphoria of yesterday has now evaporated a bit, but it's difficult to say, we just don't know. I still think they might all traipse back into camp at lunch time, laughing at us, or they're all gone and that's it.

But by midday I was plunged into gloom once more:

It's snowing right across K2 now and high up the winds are picking up again. Through the big Austrian binoculars two of the high-altitude porters who've got extremely good eyesight, Michael and I have failed to pick up any sign of movement on the one bit of the Abruzzi between Camps 2 and 3 that is visible from Base Camp. Above that the route is round the corner and so it is below, but it's hard to imagine anyone above House's Chimney being able to move on a day like this and particularly not when you consider the condition of utter exhaustion that all seven must by now be in.

By evening our worries were focused on Janusz, Anna and Krystyna who should have been down from the Negrotto Col by then.

We lost radio contact completely with Janusz. The six o'clock call didn't come through and we walked up the Strip in a grim, horrible sort of Welsh evening, a thick mist down and drizzling—no sign of them. At eight o'clock they finally came through and I don't know what they've spent the day doing. They must be absolutely on their last legs, but they're now down on the glacier looking for the old American Camp 1 which is really just a few hundred feet above Casarotto's crevasse, and all being well they should be down some time to-morrow morning. It's a vile night. I just can't see how the others higher up can be surviving all this. I hope I'm wrong.

It snowed heavily during the night and

Friday, 8th August brought no respite, visibility was down to a hundred metres. By now I had decided that all seven of them must have been caught in the weather at or below the summit and had not made it back to Camp 4. Had they done so, and managed to get brews and food inside them, surely at least a couple of the seven would have made it back down to Base Camp. My tape diary summed up the grim conclusion:

> I think for the sake of clinging on to hopes, another two or three days should see it through, but I'm now fairly convinced in my own mind that Al, Julie, Kurt, Mrufka and the three Austrians are probably all dead.

But the day was to have one good moment. By midmorning we could pick out Janusz and the girls through the binoculars, then, as they descended to Casarotto's crevasse, with the naked eye. Michael, Przemyslaw, Peter and I set off to meet them. I carried the camera and tripod, to record what might well be the last happy event of the season.

Standing by the little glacial pool at the foot of the scree slope that I had descended with Kurt after Renato's death, I watched the two girls and Janusz descending. Despite their heavy sacks, they looked, with their slightly old-fashioned clothing and equipment, like a group of youth hostellers coming down from the Snowdon Horseshoe. The girls seemed even smaller than I remembered and coming up the slight rise from the bottom of the slope and onto the moraine of the glacier they all had to stop several times on this one last bit of uphill. Hugs all round and temporarily my spirits lifted once more. Now five had escaped the storm. Was it too much to pray for more?

Soon everyone was clustered in the frame tent brewing and eating and recounting the events of the last days. Glancing out of the door my heart leapt as I spotted a group of figures appear at the end of the Strip. Oh fantastic, it must be them! Quickly I assembled my camera on the tripod to film their arrival and zoomed in to frame and focus the figures, now only about 300 metres away, and abruptly my joy was shattered. It was a group of

Korean porters. They had just been up to do a carry back from Advance Base. As they came past, they told us that they had not seen any sign of life on the Abruzzi.

That evening I once again walked up the Strip with the Austrians' binoculars. At the edge of the glacier I systematically scanned the huge avalanche cones at the foot of the Abruzzi where Liliane's body had been found, to no avail. Then I slowly examined the pinnacles, buttresses and snowslopes that made up the bottom third of the Abruzzi. Above House's Chimney was a long snowslope, and in the middle of it were three tiny dots, two quite close together and a third higher up. Intently I stared as the cloud base, which was at more or less the same level, shifted. Sometimes the specks were clear, sometimes they vanished. Were they moving? or were they just boulders?

As the light faded I retraced my steps. I remembered that on Kongur in 1981 I had spent ten days with Michael Ward at Advance Base, sitting out a storm and, when it had cleared, waiting anxiously for the return of Pete Boardman, Joe Tasker, Chris Bonington and Al. We had finally spotted them on a snowslope on the day that Michael and I both knew was probably the last one before we would have to assume there had been an accident of some sort. Could history repeat itself?

With the Poles safe, I was now desperately eager to get up to Advance Base and at least see the bottom section of the Abruzzi for myself. I had thought long and often about the possibility of some sort of search but knew it would almost certainly be a waste of time. There was no-one at Base Camp who could get high on the mountain, except those who had recently done so, and they were in no fit state to return so soon. There was no question of anyone being able to reach Camp 4 in any case. To go to 8000 metres in the storm, even if possible, would probably just add to the casualty list. Actually to be able to effect a rescue was also unlikely. If any survivors were incapable of getting themselves down, it would take a huge rescue team to do it. I knew enough about mountain rescue not to have any illusions on that score. Even the Americans with Art Gilkey in 1953 knew that their heroic attempt to get him down was really only a gesture. I considered just trying to go up the ropes on my own and see how far I could get. Realistically this would only be to assuage my conscience and tell relatives I had at least done something. But, of course, all my hill gear had been sent back. Could I borrow some? I was by far and away the biggest person at Base Camp, and would never get into the Koreans' gear, let alone double boots, and even the Poles were all smaller than I.

But I could at least go to Advance Base and spend the night there. If I returned on the 10th without any signs of anyone that would be the final confirmation that they had all perished. At Base Camp I asked Michael Messner if he would come with me. I felt for him, for not only was he in the same position as I, but he was on his first Karakoram expedition and still in his early twenties. He seemed even more shocked by events than I was. He was expecting their porters for the return journey to arrive any day now and was in a desperate quandary about letting all the gear go and whether or not he should go with it. We agreed to go up to Advance Base the following day but he would not stay the night. This suited me, for I felt a strong need to be on my own for a while. I mentioned the three dots I had seen but by now it was too dark to pick them out from Base Camp.

In the morning I went down and tried to explain to Michael exactly where I had seen what I hoped were survivors. Once more the cloud base was low but occasionally lifted a bit. I couldn't pick anything out, which of course gave me cause for optimism, for if there had been figures coming down they would not be visible now.

We set off for Advance Base. Michael, built like a greyhound, would be much faster than I, so I left first, arranging to wait for him at the bottom of the short icefall. As I approached the first flat section of the glacier there was a noise like an electric train and a colossal avalanche cloud suddenly swept out of the mist above and billowed out and down onto the glacier. I threw my rucksack off and ran, but the cloud subsided before it reached me and shamefacedly I retraced my steps. At the foot of the icefall and under the second huge avalanche cone I used the binoculars to search the fresh debris. With their magnification I realised that the slopes were littered with bits and pieces that had been swept down from above. Aluminium tent poles, stuff bags, bits of material, lengths of rope, a torn sleeping bag: none of it looked recent and the colours of the remnants seemed faded and bleached. The cloud was well below House's Chimney and the snowslope I had seen the dots on the night before was hidden. Michael arrived, relieved I had not been caught in the avalanche, and we entered the maze of the icefall. It was still marked with flags on bamboo poles that had been left by the French. Occasionally a flag of ancient vintage would appear at some odd angle, far off route, showing how the icefall had changed. It was all dry ice, and complex rather than dangerous. With no need to rope up, Michael soon pulled ahead. Predictably, I then got mildly lost, following flags that led nowhere and failing to spot a diversion to my left.

With mounting apprehension we climbed the last hundred metres of moraine to the site of Advance Base. There was no-one there. Amidst the debris of abandoned food, packing cases and litter, was one small olive green hooped tent. It was Kurt and Julie's. Inside were two big locked drums, presumably film gear, and more scraps of food. Michael and I sat down and carefully scanned the ridge through the binoculars. Only the tents of Camp 1 were visible, high above. Nothing stirred. Beyond them the characteristically orange-coloured buttress containing House's Chimney appeared and disappeared in the clouds. Spindrift blew past like smoke. Michael stayed for a snack, then, concerned at the possible arrival of his porters, set off down.

I suppose I only stayed the night as a gesture, but it seemed the right thing to do. I spent the rest of the afternoon examining every inch of what bits of the ridge were visible. I could follow the line of fixed rope most of the way to Camp 1 and occasionally above it. The snowslopes at the bottom of the ridge were embedded with gas cartridges and various containers dropped from above. Once more, nothing was new or cast any light on what might have happened. I remembered Kim had told me that Al and Mrufka had slept under a big boulder near Advance Base and I descended to the most likely one on the moraine. Sure enough, on the far side an overhang formed a sort of cave and rocks had been shifted to make a flat space. A rucksack was lying there containing a sweater and a few bits and pieces of spare clothing, gloves etc. I remembered that Al, after his first attempt, had left a rucksack here. But this was the one he had left Base Camp with. He must have changed them. Sadly I regarded the contents and left it where it was.

There was a Camping Gaz stove in Kurt's tent and some billies. I made a vague attempt at a meal and then, realising I had forgotten to bring a Karrimat with me, searched around in the dusk for bits of packing case to insulate the floor. The wind had got up and I was glad to get into my sleeping bag.

All night long the tent flapped and rattled in the wind. I dozed uncomfortably and kept hearing voices and footsteps on the scree. Several times I undid the door and peered out, but there was no-one there. I packed up and, before I left, went down to the bottom of the moraine to a spot where melt water was gurgling out of the ice. I filled a pan and left it in the tent next to the stove with some tea bags, sugar and a cigarette lighter. Then I did the tent up and, by now rather tearfully, had one last long look through the binoculars. Above the wind blew unabated. Streamers of snow and cloud shrieked off the ridge like a forest fire. Surely no-one could possibly still be alive? Below the camp a rib of rock ran almost down to the glacier. It was, technically, the lowest point of the Abruzzi. I stopped and prised off a few fragments of rock to bring back to give to Deborah and Al's mother, Eve. Sorrowfully I picked my way down the moraine, through the icefall and across the glacier. Walking down the shifting moraines at the far end of the Strip I kept hearing voices again, and climbed up the scree to look. No-one there. Perhaps I'm going mad, I thought, but couldn't summon up much enthusiasm to pursue the subject. Later Michael told me that he too had imagined voices which showed that I was not alone. Perhaps he was going mad as well.

Before I got to the Strip I noticed a couple of Koreans. They were examining something and beckoned me over. It was a human femur, bleached by the sun. Near to it were a few shreds of clothing. Earlier on, Phil Burke and Al Burgess had made an even more macabre find on the traverse round the rocky spurs to the Savoia Glacier: two withered fingers with blackened flesh still clinging to the bones. They were almost certainly the remains of a porter who had been killed in almost the same place on Reinhold Messner's 1979 expedition. But the femur was a mystery. Its position, well onto the glacier, suggested it had taken many years to get there. Possibly Dudley Wolfe, or one of the Sherpas who tried to rescue him, I thought with a shudder. Best to leave it where it was, but I noticed later with irrational distaste the Koreans bringing it back to Base Camp.

Rather more fascinating was the find the Austrians had made earlier on. This was a broken ice axe, its shaft was only about six inches long and the head, intact though twisted, still had the clear imprint of "Ashenbrenner Innsbruck". This could easily have been one of Art Gilkey's belaying axes when he was swept away by the avalanche. The two huge couloirs at the foot of the Abruzzi naturally funnelled everything down the mountain from the Shoulder and above; the axe had come down the one below the Gilkey Couloir.

Plodding back over the glacier, the weather had improved slightly and I could now see the snowslope above House's Chimney quite clearly. There were still three dots there, they hadn't moved and were obviously rocks.

At Base Camp a party of English trekkers had just arrived. Whooping with delight at reaching journey's end, they were in a high good humour. I found it hard talking to them. It seemed unfair to burden them with my problems and ruin their day, yet I couldn't help feeling resentful that they could simply wander into this situation and leave it again a couple of hours later. But they were very sympathetic and helpful, and their presence forced all of us at Base Camp to consider very carefully what to do next.

Porters and trekkers in the area would have heard on the grapevine that there had been a big storm on K2 with possibly the loss of many lives. Even now rumours would be flowing out to Askole and from there to Skardu. Inevitably the press would get wind of it and reports and rumours would hit the outside world. How could we try to ensure that the news was suppressed until we knew for certain that it was accurate? First I asked the trekkers not to say anything to anyone, which they of course agreed to. Then Capt. Neer (who was proving himself to be easily the most understanding and caring Liaison Officer at Base Camp) asked Michael and me into his tent to discuss what to do.

"Mr. Jim, you are older and more experienced, you must advise us on the situation."

You must be joking I thought, if you think this happens to me every year! We tried to think what to do for the best. First we would get a message to the helicopter base at Gore to ask for one to come up and, at its maximum altitude, at least examine the lower slopes of the Abruzzi. This again would be something of a gesture but, if anyone *was* descending, the helicopter would give them hope and we could set out to meet them. Then we agreed to send out a telex via Skardu giving the names of those missing. This would go on the first helicopter that arrived and in this way the news should have reached the outside world before the rumours.

Finally the Captain asked me if I would take responsibility for Kurt and Julie's equipment.

"You understand what to do with the filming gear, and of course Julie is English." He was right, but I hated the thought of breaking into their tents and making decisions about what to keep and what to throw away. One thing I had to do was retrieve the two drums of film equipment still at Advance Base. None of the Koreans' porters seemed interested in doing any carrying and earning some extra money. I was sitting outside my tent wondering what to do when a familiar and not very welcome figure approached.

It was Ghulam, my erstwhile film porter. As if nothing had happened, he squatted beside me and asked after my health! He had just arrived with a Japanese trekker. His eyes flickered round as he tried to assess what could be bartered for.

"You have sleeping bag?"

"Yes, Ghulam, I have, and it's for me to sleep in."

The heavy sarcasm was wasted. Suddenly I had an idea and asked Ghulam if he would do a carry from Advance Base. As if by magic his brother materialised from thin air and they both agreed to go up first thing in the morning.

"Remember," I told Ghulam forcefully, "you *must* leave the tent. Do you understand?"

"I think everyone now dead." Ghulam's reply was ambiguous.

"I don't give a shit what you think. *You must leave the tent.* Understand?"

"Yes, yes, I will leave the tent."

I couldn't bring myself to go through Kurt and Julie's tent and put it off until the following morning. That evening, I resigned myself to the inevitable: they had now been gone for twelve days, which was exactly double Al's estimate. They had taken food and fuel for six days, and I knew that all hope was gone for Al and

Mrufka, Kurt and Julie and the three Austrians.

I awoke on the morning of the 11th with the strange, but certain feeling that Al was now dead. I didn't know why but I was convinced that there was no hope left. I found that I could face sorting out his gear without feeling as though I was committing a crime. It was made easier by Al's avowed intention to sell most of it on his return. I kept personal things and ruthlessly made a pile of the rest to sell. Apart from anything else I needed to raise every rupee I could to pay for the return trip, for Al seemed to have far less cash than he had thought and it was strewn all over the tent. I steeled myself to find his passport and look through whatever documents related to the expedition. I found some letters from home and finally uncovered his spare glasses and cleaning fluid for his contact lenses. These last two I couldn't cope with and I wept bitter tears.

Then I forced myself to go to Kurt and Julie's tent and do the same. In the middle of sorting out what was obviously going to be a much bigger job, I suddenly heard the faint but unmistakable drone and clatter of a helicopter. Was it coming to search? It landed and out jumped what was obviously a high-ranking officer; a colonel I soon found out. Officiously he marched through the Base Camp tents while the two Liaison Officers shouted orders to porters and cooks. The helicopter lifted off and to my consternation wheeled away and back down to Concordia. For Christ's sake, what was going on?

The colonel had arrived to buy anything he could lay his hands on from the Koreans. Soon a car-boot sale was going on as duvet jackets, stoves, gas cylinders and all kinds of bits and pieces of equipment were displayed. Krystyna and Anna were understandably incensed and tried to ask the colonel whether a helicopter was going to try and search. Being women, they were ignored and the colonel, a caricature of a big and incredibly stupid army bully with high black boots and a crew-cut, dismissed them curtly.

Summoning up what little self-control I had I introduced myself and tried to turn the conversation to K2.

"I am here with my camera but I cannot get a good photograph of K2 with all the cloud." He seemed quite irate that the mountain should behave this way.

It was the cloud, I explained, that was the problem, for inside it seven of our friends were lost. Could the helicopter at least fly to the foot of the Abruzzi and see if there were any signs of life? This, I learnt, would need special permission from the authorities. Also turbulence could cause a crash. All we were asking was that it flew up on the glacier for less than five minutes and circled round and back, but I was wasting my time. Eventually the helicopter returned and loaded up the swag before leaving us, fuming with frustration.

"Perhaps," Janusz suggested, "if we tell them that there is a sleeping bag for sale near the summit of K2 they will return."

The colonel had at least taken with him a message I had written, announcing the names of all the missing climbers who were presumed dead in the storm. As the helicopter left I realised with horrible clarity that I had just thrown a stone into a pond whose ripples would spread all over the world, causing grief and misery to friends, parents, wives and husbands.

I returned to Kurt's tent and discovered a large plastic container of home brewed lager that was almost untouched. It seemed a shame to waste it, so I carried it over to the Polish tent, and then returned to carry on my desultory sorting. At last I found what I needed—Kurt and Julie's passports and some money to pay for their gear to be taken at least to Skardu. I hoped I was doing all the right things. I was worried that the porters, who by now were arriving to collect the Austrian and Korean gear, would rifle the contents of the tents so, feeling even more like a thief, I took the money and hid it in my tent. Then, having had enough for one day, I went over to the Polish tent and we had a meal and a mug of lager each. Krystyna proposed a toast "to all our friends on the mountain" and we drank silently.

There was a sudden commotion outside and a porter ran past.

"The Baltoro Marathon," said Przemyslaw casually.

I glanced out of the tent door. There in the twilight, coming along the Strip, was a small figure, staggering, stumbling and swaying from side to side. We gazed in awe and horror, stunned by the sight, as we realised that approaching us through the dusk was a survivor of the holocaust.

4

POLES, Koreans, the two Liaison Officers, porters, we gathered as if by magic and ran towards the apparition. With a sharp pang of guilty disappointment I realised quickly it wasn't Al. But who? Michael Messner, wide-eyed with incredulity, whispered, "It is Willi." Supported by porters, Willi Bauer half fell into his arms. He presented a ghastly sight, face cracked and caked in dried blood, clothing tattered and soiled. He pointed feebly to his mouth gesturing both for drink and to try and explain that he couldn't speak. He was, quite literally, on his last legs. Half mobbed by frantic helpers, he was escorted back to the Austrian tents, where a crowd bombarded him with questions that the poor man couldn't possibly understand, let alone answer.

I hung back, dreading the news and knowing crowding him wouldn't help. Through the throng I could hear names passed around: Kurt, Hannes, Alfred, Julie. At last someone, I can't remember who, got a coherent message. Julie was dead. That seemed to be a flat statement of fact. So, it seemed, were Alfred Imitzer and Hannes Wieser. Kurt was somewhere behind and Mrufka was missing . . . and Al? He was delirious and still in a tent at Camp 4, unable to move.

Even this information was confused and inconclusive. The first priority was to get to Advance Base as quickly as possible and see who, if anyone, was there. Almost as I thought this I caught sight of Ghulam furtively skulking away from the mass of curious porters. Ghulam! He had carried the loads from Advance Base late that morning. I knew straightaway what he had done.

"You bastard—you've pinched the bloody tent, haven't you?"

Ghulam cringed. "Misunderstanding," he muttered.

"F— misunderstanding!" I exploded in wrath. "If you know words as long as that you can't possibly misunderstand!"

Suppressing a strong desire to hit him, which would cause even more confusion, I returned to my tent, brain spinning as I tried to cope with the latest turn of events. To get to Advance Base was now extremely urgent. Kurt, if he had managed to get down, would naturally expect his tent to be there. Now I had taken his money, broken open his gear, drunk his lager, and indirectly, stolen his tent. Christ Almighty, I'd just announced his death to the world as well.

In my state of shock, I found myself starting to giggle. "If I'd known you cared that much about the bloody lager, Kurt, I'd have drunk it a week ago and got you down much earlier."

In my tent I tried to calm down and get my gear together: sleeping bag, Karrimat this time, all the spare clothes I could lay my hands on, medical kit. In the Base Camp tent, Janusz and Krystyna were preparing too: a tent, spare sleeping bag, what else? Radio, food, billies, stove (Ghulam would have pinched those as well). Headtorch batteries, spare gloves. Quickly we got it together and set off at about 8.30. Przemyslaw and Michael Messner were preparing to leave later.

They would go up the fixed ropes to Camp 2, or beyond, in search of Mrufka.

We walked steadily up the Strip in the dark to the glacier. The last time I had done this was for Casarotto. It seemed years ago. Would this be a repeat performance? By night our torches cast strange shadows, and even on the flat, easy section I had to think hard to remember where to go. In the dark I had a tendency to stray right, into the middle of the glacier, while Janusz and Krystyna seemed to veer off to the left. We got to the icefall without incident and for about the first hundred metres we followed the flags; then got conclusively lost.

"I don't think there's much point even trying to find the tracks, Janusz, we may as well just keep going in the right general direction."

About halfway up the icefall we stopped to change our headtorch batteries, by now very dim. But my new one quickly lost its power. Janusz, more by accident than design, found the trail near the top of the icefall and soon we were on the moraine with only about ten minutes of steep scree left before Advance Base. There was no sight or sound of anyone. Unless we had passed on the glacier, which seemed most unlikely, Kurt must still be somewhere above.

It was now 11.30. While Janusz and Krystyna started getting the tent up, I went down once more to the place where water gurgled from the ice. Now it was just a trickle. At the very foot of the Abruzzi I stared up into the darkness for any sign of a light but could see nothing. It was a moonless night but a few stars flickered in a gusty sky. Ahead a long snowslope dimly disappeared into the darkness. Some two hundred metres above was the start of the fixed ropes. I could hear a faint noise which might have been the wind flapping something; or water dripping; or just possibly someone descending. I shouted Kurt's name into the night but it didn't seem to carry and there was no reply. I started kicking steps up the easy-angled snow, occasionally stopping and listening for the noise, which was intermittent. Was I imagining things again? My headtorch was so dim it only cast a weak yellow pool of light around me. Suddenly I became aware of a dark shape moving above. As with Willi, my first feeling was of horror, fear even. The shape got nearer and, almost colliding with him, I met Kurt.

He was spread-eagled, facing into the slope, feebly kicking in his crampons, his right hand placing his axe into the snow. His head was actually resting against the snow.

"Kurt, Kurt, it's me, Jim, you're nearly safe now." We met in a clumsy embrace.

Kurt slowly registered my presence. In his heavy accent he murmured, "I have seen the lights and heard the voices, but I think I am imagining things." Then, distraught, he whispered, "I have lost Julie."

I tried to pull myself together and shouted down for help. Kurt moved slowly down under his own steam, until we reached the scree and boulder slope separating us from the site of Advance Base. It was only about fifty metres but a nightmare. Kurt, once off the even snow, was almost helpless and we had to semi-carry him and carefully place his feet. At one point he sprawled full length, luckily with no damage.

"All the way down, and now I fall for the first time."

Passing the ice-cold trickle of melt water, Kurt drank greedily. "No, Kurt, not too much, not so fast." Krystyna unsuccessfully tried to stop him. At last we reached the tents.

Krystyna and Janusz got Kurt inside the tent while I started a never-ending series of brews on the stove outside. Kurt drank anything that was going: tea, soup, chocolate. While he drank Krystyna examined his fingers and toes. Black and blistered with frostbite, they looked appalling, but we were aware that appearances could be deceptive. The important thing in the first stages is to keep the affected areas clean to stop infection and, subsequently, gangrene, setting in. Luckily, after over two months here, my small medical kit was still more or less intact and Krystyna applied antiseptic cream and bandaged Kurt's hands and feet. All the time Kurt was talking about what had happened, half in German, which Krystyna spoke, and sometimes in English. Outside the tent I couldn't really follow, but I already knew the answer to the one question I had wanted to ask. The details would come later, when Kurt was ready for them; and I could face asking him.

At last after yet more fluid intake, and managing a few small scraps of chocolate, Kurt, who had lapsed in and out of consciousness, fell asleep and I set about finding a flat space to unroll my Karrimat. It was a cold night but not snowing and I soon warmed up in my sleeping bag. I stared into the darkness above. I knew that somewhere up there Al's body would be lying, still and lifeless, but emotionally I just couldn't take it in.

I had hardly gone to sleep when the quiet of the night was broken by the arrival of Przemyslaw and Michael. Half awake, I sensed rather than saw them stop for a brew. They then carried on up to Camp 1, and I slept soundly for a couple of hours.

We all awoke at six. It was a far better day than it had been since the storm had started, though broken clouds still scudded across the Black Pyramid. The summit slopes glittered in the sun. More brews for Kurt and then Janusz opened up the radio. It was imperative to get a couple of porters up quickly with more medical kit, food, gas and above all, Kurt's moon boots, for now he could not get his feet into his climbing boots. These I noticed, with some surprise, were not plastic, which in the last few years have been almost universally adopted for alpine and Himalayan climbing, but an ancient pair of leather doubles. They were completely waterlogged and weighed a ton. Most of Kurt's gear seemed very old-fashioned, but he did have a titanium ice axe.

While we waited for the porters, Kurt fretted about what items of equipment to leave and what to carry down. He was reasonably coherent but already quite obsessively concerned with trivia. Once embarked on a line of thought he pursued it endlessly. I wondered if it was just extreme fatigue, or whether oxygen lack over a long period had affected him.

The porters must have travelled very quickly for they arrived before eight. Janusz was staying here until the search for Mrufka was completed, and Krystyna and I would get Kurt down. But the high-altitude porters, big strong Hunza lads, wanted to return immediately. They hadn't had their breakfast they explained. Once more I lost my temper.

"Can't you see this man hasn't eaten for a week. You must stay and help." One just shrugged and set off not to be seen again, the other I pushed and bullied into helping. It was obvious that even between the three of us, getting Kurt down was going to be a desperately slow and difficult business.

And so it proved. Going down the moraine to the glacier in the daylight was not as bad as I had feared. Initially I supported Kurt but as he warmed up it was easier for him to walk slowly but unaided. We evolved a technique where if a step was too difficult for him, I would use a ski stick or my own foot as a brace for Kurt. Krystyna did what she could but, being so much smaller than Kurt, it was difficult for her to support him. The porter did as little as possible but, at least, in his urgency to get down, went ahead to sort out the easiest line to follow, though I had to shout continually for him not to disappear entirely.

Once into the icefall our pace, which was already desperately slow, dropped even further. At the first difficulty, an awkward step across a crevasse and up onto a shelf on the other side, Kurt's feet shot through a snow bridge. The porter and I grabbed his wrists and Kurt gathered himself.

"One, two, three, we'll pull, and you push."

"Okay."

On the count of three nothing happened and I caught Krystyna's anxious expression behind Kurt. For a moment I seriously doubted whether he was going to get down alive. Then, summoning up every last ounce of energy, Kurt scrambled up.

The passage down through the icefall normally takes about twenty minutes. Today it took four long hours. Twice Kurt ground to a complete standstill. On the first occasion I massaged his feet and legs which he could not feel at all. This was affecting his balance. At last the blood seemed to flow again and our painful progress resumed. But not far from the end of the icefall and the beginning of the flat dry section of the glacier Kurt stopped again.

"Jim, please feel my pulse."

I pressed my fingers to his wrist, but could feel nothing at all. "Seventy," I lied confidently after a minute.

"That is good," Kurt muttered, then ominously, "I can feel that the engine is running down."

At this point I suggested Krystyna and the porter got off as quickly as possible and arranged for a stretcher party from Base Camp. I couldn't understand why every available man wasn't already here. Now, on our own and at last onto easy ground, Kurt revived a bit and we plodded painfully slowly through the afternoon sunshine which was actually hot enough for Kurt to take his down jacket off. He was talking: fragments of what had happened, but mainly reminiscing about earlier expeditions with Julie. I just listened; anything to distract him from the present colossal effort he was making to keep going.

At last to my relief, figures, like the cavalry at the end of a western, appeared on the horizon. Thank God. It proved to be members of the Australian Army Broad Peak expedition, whom I had met before.

They had come up to K2 Base Camp for a walk and to find out the latest news. They couldn't have timed it better. They had brought materials for an improvised stretcher. They were calm, capable and confident. Suddenly I felt drained and shattered. Then Kurt, who was at last in good hands, turned to me.

"Perhaps you could go on ahead to Base Camp and film me as I come in?"

You old showman, I thought, amused at his desire, even now, to play to the crowd.

"Okay. I'll shoot off two rolls, one for your film and one for mine."

Relieved of my duties, I set off quickly and, with a bit of action at last, worked off some of my pent-up tensions.

Back once more on the Strip I filmed Kurt's arrival in the early evening dusk. It *was* good footage: a feeling of disaster, purveyed through the hand held and fleeting images of stretcher bearers and helpers, all with a sense of urgency as their horizontal burden was carried the last few yards. Here the Australian and Korean doctors, who had spent the day with Willi Bauer, took over and Kurt was placed in the Poles' Base Camp tent. At last, after twenty-four hours of non-stop mental and physical exertion, I could try and unwind. But late that night Kurt insisted on going back to his own tent, some 200 metres down the Strip, and in the dark it took about another half-hour to escort him there. Finally, he managed to get into his tent and into a sleeping bag and I left him to go to sleep. I also gave him a thermos of tea, which of course he couldn't manage to open with his bandaged hands.

The next morning, I returned to Kurt's tent with a brew. I hated to wake him up and bring him back to the present, but slowly he came round. After a couple of brews he managed to eat some tinned fish and a few biscuits. Slowly, bit by bit, Kurt began to tell the story of what had happened. It took most of that day and the following one, to get the whole picture. Like Willi Bauer, Kurt was at times incoherent, confused, and tended to repeat himself. He was still desperately tired and utterly distraught at the death of Julie. Consequently I received a very fragmentary picture, in no particular chronological order, of what had happened.

He told me that he and Julie had

reached the summit very late on the 4th. I got the impression that it was about seven p.m., almost in twilight. The incoming storm had been below them all day and the sky above was clear, but there was no view from the top.

Almost as soon as they started down Julie had fallen past Kurt and they had both gone about a hundred metres before sliding to a halt. Then Julie fell again but Kurt had managed to stop her after only a short distance. They had to bivouac because, although Julie had taken care to disconnect the headtorch leads from the batteries, it didn't work. (I didn't understand whether they only had one, or had lost one, or whether neither worked.) They managed to dig out a small open snow hole above the final séracs and in the morning of the 5th, in white-out conditions, descended the Bottleneck and eventually made it to within hailing distance of Camp 4. Kurt said that Julie had been crawling for the last bit and that he was worried about finding the tents. Julie was also having trouble with her vision. At Camp 4 the others, trapped in the white-out, were still there. Willi Bauer had heard their cries and helped Julie into camp and taken her into the Austrians' tent to warm up.

As the information slowly emerged, I wished he would tell me something of what had happened to Al and Mrufka. I gathered that Mrufka had not got to the summit, and presumed that Al hadn't either. In the circumstances I didn't care much one way or the other, and it seemed a mildly irrelevant, almost insensitive, question to ask. I was more interested in why they had taken so long, and why they hadn't tried to come down. But Kurt suddenly volunteered the information that Al had indeed got to the top, and on the 4th he had led most of the way, until he was overtaken by two of the three Austrians with only about a hundred metres to go. He had told Willi Bauer and Alfred Imitzer he was relieved that someone else could break the trail for the last section. On the summit day, Kurt thought that Al had been the strongest of them all. As he told me, I couldn't help the tears falling. Of course it *was* important that he'd done it at last, and I could just visualise his big wide grin of triumph as he stood almost on the top of the world on his own. For a few short moments, all his dreams would have been fulfilled, his problems solved.

Some way behind him Mrufka had apparently stopped and actually fallen asleep in the snow. Kurt and Julie had woken her and she had carried on up, but was climbing erratically and, in Kurt's opinion, seemed on the verge of falling off. Julie had been worried that she could cause an accident but Kurt said that he had tried to reassure her and told her to see Mrufka's climbing as just another problem to overcome.

Al descended from the top and Kurt and Julie explained that they couldn't be responsible for Mrufka. There seemed to have been a "heated discussion". I wasn't clear whether it was between them all or just Al and Mrufka. It ended with Al persuading Mrufka, who must have been bitterly disappointed, that it would be folly to continue at this time of day, even though she was very close to the top. They apparently made an uneventful descent to Camp 4, while Kurt and Julie went on to the summit.

When Kurt and Julie regained Camp 4 after their bivouac, the storm, which had already hit the lower part of the mountain, broke in earnest. Julie, after being ministered to by the Austrians, had rejoined Kurt, but that night of the 5th-6th their tent was buried in snow drifting with high winds, and they had been rescued by Willi. Julie went into the Austrian tent, Kurt to Al and Mrufka's. In the afternoon of the 6th, Julie came to the door of the tent and complained that she felt very strange. Kurt told me again that her vision was badly affected. She returned to the Austrian tent, with Kurt, seemingly, unaware of how ill she was becoming. On the morning of the 7th, during a lull in the storm, Willi called over to them that Julie had died in the night.

The news came as a complete bombshell to Kurt and he was overcome with grief and remorse that he had not been with her. Al consoled him and, as Kurt told me the harrowing story, he paused to find the right word.

"Alan," he said at last, "was always a gentleman."

The gas ran out on the 8th and Al's

condition deteriorated. I got the impression that this was quite sudden. The storm continued unabated until the 10th with Al lapsing in and out of delirium, rambling and demanding water. All of them seemed to have been only semi-conscious for the last two days, and on the morning of the 10th, in limited visibility, they at last decided to get down, all except Al who was still talking about melting water in his sleeping bag and could not be persuaded to move. So they had left him. Kurt believed that Al could not possibly have lasted the night.

I asked Kurt if there was any possibility of Al, left on his own, having one last realisation of his situation, and perhaps by some miracle, getting it together to come down. Kurt made no reply but shook his head.

Willi and Mrufka started first, while Kurt said his last farewells to Julie who had been placed back in their wrecked tent. He caught them up, and with Willi breaking trail through chest-deep powder snow, they somehow forced their way down to the start of the fixed ropes. Alfred Imitzer and Hannes Wieser only managed a short distance before they collapsed in the snow. Mrufka, who had been as strong or stronger than Kurt, started having trouble with her Sticht plate at this point. (A vision of Al telling her not to bother with a figure-of-eight flashed across my mind.) Willi and Kurt had gone ahead with Mrufka going slowly and not in any obvious trouble. Camp 3 had been virtually destroyed and Willi had carried on down. He reached Camp 2 first, found a stove and made a brew by the time Kurt arrived. They had slept, exhausted, but Mrufka had not arrived. Kurt seemed convinced that she had stopped at a higher tent left by Wanda earlier on.

Finally I brought up what I thought was the most important question. Why hadn't anyone followed the Koreans on the 3rd? Kurt seemed puzzled, as if it had happened long ago, which from his point of view it had. He said, vaguely, that Al and Mrufka had spent the night of the 2nd some 200 metres below his and the Korean tent, and had moved up to be with him, so as to make an early start on the 4th. They had spent the day of the 3rd resting and brewing. He didn't say why he and

Julie, or Willi, Alfred and Hannes had not followed the Koreans. I supposed they might all have been suffering from a feeling of euphoria which suppressed any sense of urgency. Or perhaps in that atmosphere of suppressed competition, no-one could bring themselves to suggest retreat? I asked Kurt about the weather and the signs of it changing which at Base Camp had seemed so obvious, but once again he was uncommunicative. I did not push it, but I wondered if Kurt was already finding it hard to admit that he had made an error of judgement.

Throughout the day I sat and listened to or chatted to Kurt. I visited Willi, but he spoke almost no English and was in far more pain from his injuries. Earlier on the expedition I had noticed big Willi Bauer, with his balding reddish hair, around Base Camp. He looked older than his forty-five years, and reminded me of Paul Nunn, both in build and appearance. But it was hard to imagine him as a climber. He moved so slowly and deliberately and seemed withdrawn and taciturn. Now he had emerged as the strong man and had, almost unbelievably, spent *ten days* at or above 8000 metres. If you had lined up every climber of each expedition and asked yourself who would survive an ordeal like this, Willi and Kurt would come at the bottom of most people's lists. But in the end their slow, plodding, energy-conserving approach must have paid off. Don Whillans had been much the same on Annapurna and Everest, I remembered. I had poured scorn on Willi's appearance early in the trip, saying he looked as if he should be selling kiss-me-quick hats on Blackpool pier. How wrong I was.

All day we waited for news from Advance Base. Had Przemyslaw and Peter got to Mrufka? At six the sad news came. There was no sign of her. For the two girls, Anna and Krystyna, it was a cruel blow. "We feel we have lost her twice," Krystyna explained that evening.

Mrufka, like Willi and Kurt, had had badly frostbitten fingers. Whether she made a mistake on the change-over on the fixed ropes and fell off, or collapsed and died of exhaustion, or tried to descend without clipping the Sticht plate into the ropes, was a matter for futile conjecture. But she had not made it down to the Polish tent. So Mrufka, after surviving the ordeal of Camp 4, became the fifth and last victim of the storm, and the thirteenth on K2 in a single summer.

All through the day we waited for a helicopter to arrive. The colonel had said he would organise one two days before, but in apparently perfect flying weather none had come. Capt. Neer, sensing the urgency of the situation, decided to walk down to the army base at Concordia and speed things up.

I tried to impress upon him the fact that news of the disaster would make headlines all over the world. Now Kurt and Willi, having undergone one of the most incredible survival ordeals in mountaineering history, were being put in further danger as every day passed without the arrival of a helicopter. The Pakistani army would get no credit if, through the delay, more damage was done. Willi's hands were already infected and the Korean doctor was forced to cut some of the flesh away: Willi's cries of pain were terrible to listen to.

To my relief the Australian doctor and a couple of their team arrived in the afternoon and took over the job of packing Kurt's film gear. I needed to be by myself for a while, and decided to visit our old campsite across La Manche to make sure that it was cleared up. Every step of the way had subtly changed since Al and I had carried our sacks of tinned meat across to the Strip, evidence of the inexorable movement of the glacier; a huge perched block on an ice pedestal that had offered us two or three boulder problems had fallen; even the rivulets and melt channels from the Savoia Glacier were different. It was like walking through a house after someone had changed the furniture around. Ascending the moraine leading to our site was almost dangerous with the risk of large blocks sliding down the underlying ice.

The campsite was picked clean, by porters, birds, and presumably the little guinea pig-like animals that had lived there all summer. Apart from the ashes of our last fire, there was hardly any evidence of our having been there at all. It seemed like a dream from a long-lost past; hard to believe I had only left fourteen days before. I went over to Abruzzi Close. Al's tent platform looked out to Broad Peak and down to Concordia and Chogolisa. A few scraps of rubbish littered the site, which I made a desultory attempt to clean up.

Out of sight of everyone I sat on a rock and sobbed my grief for Al. Not with any great hope that my prayers would be received by anyone, let alone answered, I prayed that Al hadn't suffered and was now at peace. Feeling a bit hypocritical, for it was the first time I had bothered the Almighty in years, I did the same for the others, realising to my shame that there were now so many I couldn't offhand remember all the names. Finally, and much more selfishly, I prayed that I would get out of this place and that some porters would turn up to help me do so.

Returning to the Strip I noticed a long line of porters coming up from Broad Peak. An instant conversion was quickly foiled by the discovery that they were for the Poles and there weren't any spare ones for me.

On the 14th more porters arrived for the Koreans, and suddenly there were more porters than loads. I was able to pick and choose. Kurt's film gear was whittled down to three loads and I got away with two. We could just afford it. In the afternoon the sound of a helicopter at last filled the air and soon the big green dragonfly was perched on the Strip some hundred metres from Kurt's tent. Kurt, with one arm round my neck and using a crutch which must have been part of the Korean's medical equipment, hobbled down to it. Michael Messner similarly supported Willi. From the air we must have looked like victims of a shipwreck. The one remaining Liaison Officer ran to the helicopter and talked to the pilot. He beckoned: to us, I thought, but as we moved forward a porter rushed past with a small rucksack and threw it into the cockpit. I watched, aghast, as the Liaison Officer got in and the helicopter rose, turned and flew off. I was trembling with rage and shouted four-lettered abuse as it disappeared from view. We returned to the tents.

That evening, the last at Base Camp, I brought the last bottle of champagne over to the Polish tent. Janusz produced a bottle of "sherry". Like every other Polish drink I have ever tasted it was about 140 per cent proof and any resemblance to its name was in the colour, an evil murky dark brown. We drank it, and the champagne, with no great enthusiasm, and stumbled off to bed feeling flat and depressed.

Up at six and an incredible dawn, ice cold and crystal clear. Two big black ravens were hopping noisily about in front of the tents scavenging bits of rubbish I had thrown out the night before. I remembered one of the twins had told me that when the Sherpas die they believe they return as goraks, the crows that will follow expeditions as high as the South Col of Everest in search of food. I studied the birds for any sign of recognition, then shooed them away. They flapped heavily out of range and eyed me frostily. I wasn't convinced.

In the early morning light, K2, catching the first rays of the sun, towered above, brilliant and ethereal. Quickly tents were struck and packed, my own two porter loads suddenly looking very meagre. The Polish porters had already gone, and so had Janusz and his team. Now only a few Koreans, Michael Messner, Kurt, Willi and a cook were left, still waiting for the helicopter.

The worst moment of all approached. As I chivvied and argued with the porters I tried not to think about it. The film loads were packed and the porters departed in ones and twos. Then Kurt called me over to his tent.

"Sit here for a few minutes, please." Kurt, at the entrance of his tent, was still transfixed by the sight of K2. "Look—on the Polish Spur—do you see that sérac? With the sunlight it seems like a gigantic fairy castle." He turned to me, tears streaking his worn cheeks. "Tell Terry that Julie and I have climbed our 'mountain of mountains'. I did not imagine it would end like this—it was Destiny that took Julie away."

I nodded dumbly.

A porter approached. "You want to sell mattress?"

"F— off," I shouted through my tears.

"GO-A-VAY," yelled Kurt.

At last I picked up my sack. "See you then, Kurt. Good luck and I hope the helicopter comes today." And I took the first step back to civilisation.

As I left and walked on my own past Broad Peak, K2 slowly assumed its true proportions and actually seemed to grow as I got further away. Every time I looked back the summit seemed higher, and more and more remote. But as I approached Concordia a bank of cloud drifted around the mountain. Impatiently I waited for the porters, whom I had overtaken, for I wanted one last shot. By the time they arrived the cloud ceiling stretched unbroken across the valley. This time I was going to sit it out. I waited for an hour but was just deciding to go, when suddenly impossibly high in the sky the black rocks at the top of the South-South-West Ridge, the "Magic Line", emerged from the clouds. Through the viewfinder the summit snows glinted briefly. As I completed the shot, the vision receded once more into the mists and I turned for the last time and looked down the Baltoro to the distant jagged skyline of Paiju and the Cathedrals. Beyond them, Askole, Skardu, Islamabad and home.

Part Three

The Reckoning

1

THE next day at Urdokas I sat on grass for the first time in months, absorbing the sound of insects and the overwhelming vibrancy of the colour green on my retina, deprived for so long of the sight of living, growing things. I heard the sound of a helicopter coming down from Gore. Several had already gone over but I was somehow convinced that this was Kurt and Willi, on their way at last to hospital in Skardu. As it passed I waved and, sure enough, it turned and circled low for a closer look. I caught a glimpse of an answering salute as the helicopter flew out over the glacier and, dwarfed by the Trango Towers, chattered off and out of sight.

All the way down the Baltoro the weather was fine. Rationing movie film, for I had shot far more than I had intended in the last two weeks, I just had enough for the classic views of the Mustagh Tower, Gasherbrum IV, Masherbrum and, at last, the "first" view of the Trango Towers. As I passed by I remembered what a brilliant expedition that had been Now, surely, I was seeing the grea chimney stack of the Nameless Tower for the last time. As if to confirm this I ran out of film as I got the shot that I had waited for in vain all those weeks before. But in all these last shots I was conscious that there was no-one in them, the stage was empty.

At Paiju I succumbed to a violent attack of dysentery and the miles to Askole seemed endless. When I got there I collapsed and spent a nightmarish day and night camped in pouring rain on my own in a field of mud. Racked by vomiting and stomach cramps, I could barely reach the tent door to throw up into a puddle. Then a stray dog would lap up the mess. Semi-delirious, I imagined Al was in the tent with me and, with chattering teeth or sweating profusely, I moaned the night away in a sodden sleeping bag.

The two days to Dasso were a blur of effort and misery but then my luck changed. Capt. Neer Khan had come up in a jeep from Skardu to Dasso twice in two days, so concerned had he had been for my welfare and also that of Michael Messner, who had left after Kurt and Willi's departure, but had now caught me up. So we drove down to Skardu together and I was on my way to Islamabad the day after. On the Fokker Friendship I sat next to a young army officer who waxed eloquent about the view. But I couldn't even summon the energy to take photographs as the bulk of Nanga Parbat slid past on my left.

I arrived by taxi at the British Club and was suddenly dropped back into the civilised world of families round the swimming pool. "*Don't* run, Nigel!" were the first words I heard, just before I bumped into a familiar figure making his way to the bar. It was Dave Wilkinson, who had heard the news just before he was due to fly home and had unselfishly spent two long weeks on his own, waiting for me.

A week later we were at Heathrow, then up the M1 and, at last, home, to be plunged into private and public explanations, visiting Eve and Dick (Al's mother and stepfather) and Deborah, whose baby was due at any moment, coping with my own sorrow, and re-assuring Cass and my children that I was fit and well.

As I had imagined, the press and TV had given the news immense coverage that ranged from the responsible and informed reporting of *News at Ten* (who, it must be admitted, had got a head start over the rest of the field with our previous reports), to the fantasies of the popular press about the death of Julie in particular. The British climbing world, united for once in its grief for the loss of Al and Julie, was rife with speculation and theories, not all of them pleasant. Bastions of the Alpine Club wrote critical letters to *The Times* questioning aspects of the disaster, and others replied. The one thing they had in common was a woeful lack of information and a desire for a simple solution. Thus, lack of oxygen, lack of support, lack of leadership and lack of organisation were all pinpointed as the main cause for the final tragedy. It seemed there were those who felt that something was not quite right about Kurt and Willi surviving while Al and Julie died, and there were even hints that Kurt had not reached the summit. The old guard were upset that the "spirit of the pre-war days" seemed to have gone and that people were abandoned on the descent, conveniently forgetting similar examples on Everest and elsewhere in the 'twenties and 'thirties. The feeling seemed to prevail that what had happened was indefensible.

I was appalled. I couldn't believe that distinguished mountaineers, doctors and scientists, could make such sweeping statements with so little information to base their assumptions on. Several of them knew me personally, yet none of them had bothered to check their pontificatings against my impressions. Perhaps I was growing too obsessed with K2, but truth and facts seemed to be becoming easily interchangeable with untruths and opinions.

The climbing press, which would be expected to dissect the tragedy with some degree of judgement and responsibility, had, like me, to make do with patchy, sometimes conflicting accounts with gaps in them, as the survivors recovered and remembered different things and started putting their traumatic experiences in perspective. *Mountain* and *High* did their best with what they received and emphasised that these were interim reports. *Climber*'s immediate coverage was less than adequate, but in their December issue they published an interview with Kurt Diemberger which shed some light at last on the question he had been too shocked to answer at Base Camp. What happened on 3rd August to stop him and Julie, Al and Mrufka, and the three Austrians from following the Koreans to the summit?

His story was otherwise much as he had related it to me over those last painful days reliving the nightmare at Base Camp, with one significant exception. In retrospect, Kurt had now shifted the onset of the storm and Julie's subsequent death on twenty-four hours from his first-hand account to me. The earlier dates are, however, corroborated by Willi Bauer.

As for the background to the fatal day on the 3rd, according to Kurt, the Koreans and the Austrians had struck a deal that would allow the Austrians first use of the Korean tent, in return for carrying it from Camp 3 to 4, and first crack at the summit on 2nd August. Then the Koreans would have their tent and their turn on the 3rd. It was a simple-minded scheme which just might have worked if the three Austrians had made it to the top on the 2nd, as planned, and retreated to Camp 3, as promised. But they didn't, and were, not unnaturally, unwilling to go all the way down to Camp 3 before mounting a second bid. So after "a long argument" an uncomfortable logistical compromise left two of them sharing the Koreans' tent on the night of the 2nd and, when Kurt and Julie refused to accommodate the third, he went in with Al who, after such a disturbed and over-crowded night, was in no mood to try for the summit himself next day.

As for Kurt and Julie, they were put off by the lateness of the Koreans in getting away to do the oxygen-assisted trail-breaking which all the other climbers were, in varying degrees, relying on. The Austrians for their part felt they needed a day to recover, even though they were going to remain at near 8000 metres. So this, Kurt explained, was how seven people set out for the summit, which five of them achieved, on the 4th, instead of the 3rd, and by being one crucial day later found themselves so desperately immured at Camp 4 when the storm arrived in the night.

Neither Kurt, nor Willi, nor the Koreans had mentioned any of this at Base Camp. Indeed, both Willi and the Koreans had expressed bewilderment that Kurt, Julie, Al and Mrufka had not followed the Koreans on the 3rd. Apart from anything else, given the communication problems with the Koreans, I find it difficult to visualise the tent deal being struck and fully understood by either party.

Climber, in its summing up, made an ill-judged attempt at apportioning blame and praise, casting the Austrians as selfish villains and Al as the selfless hero who not only took in an Austrian overflow on the night of the 2nd, but two of the Poles coming down from the summit on the night of the 3rd, and then, as Kurt put it in his movingly stilted English: "This brave man, after two such nights, broke the trail next day to within a hundred metres of the summit, showing incredible understanding, helpfulness and endurance."

This does conveniently ignore the fact that of all the climbers in Camp 4 at the time, Al and Mrufka were the ones who actually had no right to be on the Abruzzi Ridge in the first place, but it's a good tribute and Al certainly pulled his weight.

So. Thirteen deaths on K2. How did they happen? Two in an avalanche (Pennington and Smolich); four in falls (Maurice and Liliane Barrard, Tadeusz Piotrowski and Wojciech Wröz); one in a crevasse fall (Casarotto); four from exhaustion and/or cerebral oedema (Rouse, Tullis, Imitzer, Wieser), one from rock fall (Mohammad Ali) and one unknown (Mrufka).

What kind of expeditions were the victims on? Pennington and Smolich were on a traditional fixed-rope expedition. Maurice and Liliane a small but not totally alpine-style expedition, for they had used fixed ropes and established camps. Piotrowski *was* on a genuine alpine-style push. Wröz was on a largely fixed-rope expedition. Casarotto was soloing. Imitzer, Rouse, Tullis, Wieser, Mrufka and

Mohammed Ali were all on the Abruzzi climbing it in more or less expedition style, with fixed ropes and camps, but of course not as a single expedition. Not much to be deduced from that.

Had the accidents anything in common? Maurice, Liliane, Renato, Al, Julie and Wojciech did seem to have one thing in common. All had been to the Karakoram or K2 before and all stated at some time or other that this was going to be their last attempt on the mountain. There was, in my opinion, an element of "the last throw of the dice" at work. I believe all of them saw climbing K2 as the crowning moment of their Himalayan careers. Failure would be difficult to contemplate and harder to accept. It does seem to me that over-ambition played a significant part in some of the disasters.

What else had the accidents in common? Exhaustion seemed to be a major cause though of course you don't actually die of it. Maurice and Liliane, Piotrowski and Wröz, finally fell to their deaths while descending from the summit, but all were in a state of near total exhaustion if not collapse. Michel Parmentier described to me how he had to *drag* Maurice the last few metres to the summit and how, back in the top bivouac, Maurice had been hallucinating and semi-delirious in the night. Piotrowski of course had trouble with his crampons but it also seemed that this was caused by exhaustion compounded by lack of liquid and three bivouacs without a sleeping bag; equally, exhaustion must have been the main contributory factor in Wojciech's abseiling off the end of a rope. What of the others? For Julie, Al, Hannes and Alfred it is self-evident that they must have been exhausted but their deaths were surely caused by a combination of oxygen and fluid lack. Mrufka's death must remain a question mark.

Only Al Pennington and John Smolich's deaths seem to have been "bad luck", though a sterner critic could say that to be caught in an avalanche implies a lack of judgement. Mohammed Ali comes into the same sort of category. It was a single falling stone and it killed him outright. But he was on dangerous ground at the end of a long spell of fine weather and the lower half of the Abruzzi is notoriously prone to stonefall in such conditions. Casarotto's death seemed to have been a terrible error of judgement made by a broken man who was obviously in a mental turmoil, if not actually physically exhausted.

Could the accidents have been foreseen? Simplistically the answer is an obvious no for if they could they would not have happened. *Should* they have been foreseen? Here the answer is far more complex. There seems to me to be a tendency for climbers (particularly in the upper echelons) to take a rather schizophrenic view of their abilities. Kurt Diemberger's comment to me as I left Base Camp sums it up very nicely.

"We climbed our mountain of mountains. Destiny took Julie away."

Is this a coded way of saying, "Through our skill, experience and determination we succeeded, but then had some bad luck that we could do nothing about"? This is a mountaineering parallel to the motorist's defence, "I was just driving along minding my own business when this car pulled out in front." In other words there is a strong temptation to give yourself the credit when everything is going well, but blame fate, the weather or other people when it isn't.

Different people allow different margins for error, and repetition will strengthen learned habits. Thus a cautious climber, who has often backed off in the face of bad weather, will be more inclined to do the same next time. Conversely a bolder climber will remember that last time he pressed on and got away with it, so, given a similar situation, he'll do it again. Only serious misfortune, old age and infirmity, or death, will ever change the pattern, for by definition *every* climber's experience always works in his favour, until it doesn't. Don Whillans was often quoted by Al Rouse as saying, "If you ever kill yourself on a mountain it just invalidates all your past success." I am not sure that it is quite as simple as that, but I understand the point.

On K2 several of the accidents involved people doing what had worked out for them before. In particular the Eastern Europeans have a record of frequently "going for it" without bivouac gear, sleeping bags and stoves: something that British climbers would find hard to accept.

Yet the Czechoslovakians and Poles have had a fine record of success and presumably tend to see this as the norm, not the exception.

For Kurt Diemberger the idea of arriving late on a summit is one that seems to have deep and romantic roots. He had arrived in the very last minutes of daylight on the summit of Broad Peak with Hermann Buhl in 1957. It was a profound experience and one that in *Summits and Secrets* acquires an almost mystical significance. Twenty-six years later he reclimbed Broad Peak with Julie Tullis and again, almost reliving the experience, arrived late in the day at half past six and once more descended in the dark. So Kurt seemed to have no qualms about carrying on late in the day on K2, indeed almost to relish the spiritual uplift that he and Julie gained on the summit. But this time it didn't work out.

For Kurt to admit that he has made an error of judgement seems (as it often had done with Al as well) almost impossible. Instead, in his article in *Climber* he attempts, in my view almost subconsciously, to change his perception of events, suggesting he reached the summit "between 5.30 and six" not, as he had told me, seven, while "twilight", according to him now, had gone back to eight p.m., giving them two and a half hours of daylight to get down in. In fact, Kurt says in *Summits and Secrets*, and Julie reinforces in her book, *Clouds from Both Sides*, twilight falls in the Karakoram at 6.30–7.00 p.m., and by eight it is undoubtedly pitch dark. With the storm moving in it would be dark relatively earlier. By divorcing the arrival on the summit and nightfall and, as we have seen, postponing the storm twenty-four hours, Kurt keeps his ascent of K2 as an unqualified success. Frequently on his return to Base Camp Kurt repeated that he and Julie had made an uneventful ascent of K2 and would have got down in perfect safety but for the unexpected arrival of the storm.

Turning to Al who, if he said it once, must have said a hundred times that you don't rest at 8000 metres, he had broken his rule: the rule that he knew Maurice and Liliane had already paid for with their lives. Why did he seem to be deliberately courting disaster?

Knowing Al, I suspect that his line of thought on the 3rd may have gone something like this. "I have had no sleep and I can't possibly make it to the summit today, even following in the Koreans' footsteps. If I try, and fail, I've definitely blown it. Kurt and Julie are still here, and the three Austrians. If I go down now and they do it I'll regret it all my life. So we'll camp next to them, and wait and see. After all, we can always go down if the weather turns today." Such a scenario would then surely reinforce Kurt and Julie's belief that with Al still obviously determined to try for the top their chances would still be good.

But what of the Austrians? Willi, Alfred and Hannes had descended to Camp 4 on 2nd August and had already been there two days. If they made an attempt on the 4th it would be *four* nights at 8000 metres. By having a rest day and a second attempt, they were significantly loading the dice against their own survival.

It must not be forgotten that only ten years ago it was still questionable whether or not Everest, K2 and Kangchenjunga were climbable without using oxygen, though Campagnoni and Lacedelli actually completed the first ascent of K2 without oxygen which had been used up before the final summit slopes were gained. However, since Messner and Habeler's oxygen-free ascent of Everest in 1978, all three mountains have been climbed frequently without its use. Such is the state of the art that in 1986 only the Koreans used oxygen on their summit bid. It would be tedious to bring up all the pro- and anti-oxygen arguments yet again, for they are well known. But it is a fact that above 8000 metres survival without oxygen is strictly limited, and an oxygen-free ascent of the big three is right on the limits of human capability, *whatever the circumstances*.

Twenty-seven people climbed K2 in 1986, twenty-four without oxygen. Of the thirteen fatalities, eight occurred at or above 8000 metres and oxygen lack may be reasonably claimed to be a major contributory factor in all of them. Perhaps climbers are now adopting too cavalier an attitude to the highest mountains? When Messner and Habeler climbed Everest in 1978 it was hailed as a superhuman performance but now many climbers, who are not by any stretch of the imagination superfit athletes, feel they too can do it. And the trouble is they *can*: but the cost is far too high.

In November 1986 I was invited to a symposium in Chamonix run by the French Himalaya Club. Here, to my great pleasure, I met Michel Parmentier and Benoît Chamoux, and also Norman Dyhrenfurth who later told me about a conversation he had had with Julie soon after she and Kurt had retreated from the ice traverse above the Bottleneck on their first summit bid, spending in the process four days at or above 8000 metres. On their return to Base Camp she had confided that she had decided not to have another attempt and that she was worried about Kurt, fearing he might have suffered slightly from cerebral oedema on their last attempt. It seems quite extraordinary, if that was the case, that the pair of them should have seriously contemplated going up again. Diemberger, in a letter to the *Alpine Journal*, however, claims that when he and Julie set out on their last climb, "We were in top form!"

Mental and emotional preparedness are

as important as physical form. Talking to Benoît, he made the interesting and I think valid point that whereas on his ascent *everything* was going in his favour, particularly his mental control and well-being, he felt that Al might well have been distracted by many intruding external pressures like the responsibility of looking after Mrufka, the language difficulties, the problems of being on the Abruzzi in the first place, the disappointment of failing on the North-West Ridge, the despair of returning home unsuccessful. All these could in some way have affected his judgement, to the point where just one or two wrong decisions could have tipped the scales that balanced life and death.

In February I met Janusz Majer in Scotland on the Polish visit organised by the British Mountaineering Council. We talked at length about the events of the previous year and he told me another instance of how altitude was already having an insidious effect on judgement at Camp 4. Hannes Wieser, who had decided very early on the morning of the 4th *not* to go to the top, was asked by Peter and Przemyslaw if he wanted to descend with them. He declined, saying he would wait for Willi and Alfred. In so doing, Hannes made a decision that would cost him his life. His continued presence at Camp 4 was merely consuming space, fuel and food. What possible reason was there for staying, other than a vague sense of team loyalty? Was it the same vagueness that Michel Parmentier displayed when Benoît urged him to descend? In retrospect Michel told me that he couldn't imagine why he chose to stay on his own, and Benoît said he couldn't imagine why he didn't try harder to persuade him to come down!

The use of oxygen would not, as Kurt has pointed out in his *Alpine Journal* letter, have made much difference to the final epic at Camp 4. If the Koreans had been caught in the same storm, they may well have succumbed before the others once the oxygen was finished. A far more critical factor there was fluid intake. Once the gas ran out the fluid intake ceased, blood thickened and deterioration quickly followed. And it was a factor that certainly would have affected the death of Wojciech and Piotrowski, possibly Maurice and

Liliane as well, who had also run out at their top bivouac. In the case of the Poles I do find it quite extraordinary that they could even contemplate carrying on to the summit knowing that they had no more gas. At high altitude one is supposed to drink six litres of fluid a day, which is virtually impossible to do even under ideal circumstances. To go for *three days* without any fluid is inviting disaster.

Did the mix of teams and nationalities contribute to the apparent inertia and lack of a unifying will to get away from Camp 4? They were one Pole, two Britons, but on different expeditions, and four Austrians, again from two expeditions, one of which had kept itself so fenced off from the rest of the Strip that its three members were now faced with possibly entrusting their lives to people they barely knew and, perhaps deep down, didn't trust. Added to which, there was no common language the seven could use to make a series of life or death decisions. Willi Bauer says they had agreed that they would all try and go down together or not at all (see appendix III). But no obvious leader was emerging with the necessary survival instinct to galvanise the others into action.

It is worth remembering that Janusz and Krystyna and Anna managed to descend during the storm, as did Przemyslaw and Peter Bozik. They did have a day's start, which was significant, and both groups were on fixed ropes. But the fact remains that until the 10th no-one at Camp 4 *tried* to move. Was it because no-one could really dominate the group? Or was it that everyone was too tired and befuddled to try? Or could they simply see no possibility of getting down alive?

It seemed to me at the time, and has certainly preyed on my mind since, that there were two significant periods during the storm when the opportunity might have been grabbed. The first on the morning of 5th August. There was a white-out and it was snowing but there was at that stage not much wind. Why then did no-one make a move? Were they waiting for the reappearance of Kurt and Julie? Or still exhausted from the previous summit day? Or a combination of both? Possibly even Bauer doesn't really know. After so much time at Camp 4 it is not difficult to imagine the possible torpor, half asleep and putting off any decision until something happens to force it. But Michel Parmentier had got himself down from the Shoulder in a storm and a white-out *on his own*. Had the others forgotten this? The second possibility was on the morning of the 7th. At Base Camp I commented that I could see the whole of the Abruzzi to the Shoulder and said "if anyone is up they will be, I imagine, hot-footing it down." Why then, with good visibility, even though it didn't last, was there no attempt? Sadly I fear the answer must be that Julie had died in the night and Willi had just informed Kurt, who says incidentally in one interview, that he was told during a lull in the storm. Perhaps with the trauma of Julie's death, the opportunity to go down was missed. By the morning of the 10th it was, of course, too late for all but Willi, Kurt and Mrufka.

One of the most unpleasant repercussions of the disaster was the rumour and innuendo that quickly began to make itself felt. It was not confined to Britain. In France

Michel Parmentier was virtually on trial. Instead of being praised for his heroic (but possibly unwise) wait at Camp 4, he was heavily criticised for leaving the Barrards in the first place! In Germany and Austria, controversy also raged. Kurt, perhaps unwisely, gave interviews to all and sundry. The taciturn Willi Bauer said nothing until forced to give an exclusive story to *Bunte* magazine to help pay off the expedition debts. He was then criticised for speaking out! In a much later interview in *Alpin* magazine, Bauer remains bitter about the whole media bandwagon that intruded into his private grief, and clearly is none too enamoured of Kurt, whose dramatic revelations were probably his only way of releasing his own devastated emotions. But, sadly, Kurt seemed rather too keen to apportion blame than admit his own judgement could have been at fault too. In Britain the feeling persisted that something was "not quite right", and Kurt's *Climber* interview, in my view no more than the tired ramblings of a sad and unwell man, was pounced upon by his detractors as an indication that he was concealing something.

To me it all seemed nonsensical. In an appalling disaster two people had made a quite extraordinary escape and were now being castigated for doing so. Slowly I realised that this reaction was being provoked by a deeper and more primitive anger. This was because Al, Hannes, Alfred and Mrufka *had all been left alive*. The anger was, I felt, a subconscious resentment that when put into the ultimate survival experience, Kurt and Willi in the end had to fight for their own lives, not save others.

Could this anger be a deep-rooted admission that, put in those circumstances, most of us would do the same? I was often asked would you have left Al or stayed until he died? I felt that the question was really addressed to the questioner. In my view it is not worth asking, and I am not going to criticise those unfortunate enough to have to make and live with such a decision. In Kurt and Willi's case I can only applaud their honesty in telling of what happened in the first place, and pray that it never happens to me. I can also state, with as much force as I can muster, that the condition of Willi and Kurt on their return was one of such complete and utter mental and physical collapse, that the thought of blaming them for leaving the others never even remotely crossed my mind.

As time passes and the events of 1986 slowly recede into history, one can only hope that the pain and recriminations will be blunted and some positive memories will remain, and perhaps some lessons be learnt. For it was not all bad. The Polish climbers, despite the loss of Wojciech, Tadeusz and Mrufka, did complete two outstanding new routes. The South-South-West Ridge must compare with routes like the South Face of Lhotse and the South-West Face of Everest as one of the biggest and hardest climbs in the world, and the Kukuczka-Piotrowski route was both hard, dangerous and ascended in good style. On top of that, Wanda Rutkiewicz became the first woman to climb K2, Benoît's twenty-three-hour ascent set up a speed record that will be hard to beat, and the number of K2 ascents rocketed in one summer, from a July 1985 total of thirty-nine, to sixty-six.

Inevitably the appalling death toll over-shadowed these achievements. If anything can be learnt by an analysis of all the various circumstances of each tragedy it is possible that some future mistakes may be avoided. In particular, the length of time spent at or above 8000 metres is obviously crucial, as is the need for reserves of fuel and food. The question of oxygen is still debatable. But if one thing has impressed itself on my mind throughout the last eighteen months it is that the margin for error on the world's great mountains is always slender, even under ideal conditions. Tip the scales slightly and suddenly there is no margin left. Alpine-style, oxygen-free ascents by small teams will inevitably become the norm. But a much higher proportion of unsuccessful attempts will have to be accepted as the price one pays. Otherwise the carnage will continue. Exploring and pushing the limits has always been the name of the game, whether in rock climbing, alpinism or Himalayan mountaineering. But the disas-trous summer of K2 must remain a salu-tary reminder that the limits are still there: pushing them is one thing, ignoring them another. Mountaineering will never be a safe activity and would not be worth doing if it were. But in the meteoric rise of standards, improvements in equipment and the dedication and commitment of the climbers it is all too easy to forget that the mountains never change.

K2 is not a Savage Mountain any more than the Eiger is a Killer Peak. It is an inert mass of rock, snow and ice. As I write these words, the winter winds will be howling round the Abruzzi Ridge, avalanches of powder snow will be scouring the couloirs, and the crevasses of the Savoia and the Godwin Austen Glaciers will be choked with their debris. But it will be harmless, for now there is nobody there. Humans, ambitious and ultimately fallible, will soon return to K2's bleak vastness to meet their own self-imposed challenges. I pray they will have taken heed of the events of 1986.

Appendix One

1986, The Triumphs

		Route	*Comments*
23rd June	Wanda Rutkiewicz Michel Parmentier Maurice Barrard Liliane Barrard	Polish French French French	Abruzzi Ridge	A lightweight ascent of the Abruzzi by a small team. The first female ascent of K2 by Wanda Rutkiewicz, and almost simultaneously by Liliane Barrard. Barrards lost on the descent.
23rd June	Mari Abrego Josema Casimiro	Basque Basque	Abruzzi Ridge	Two-man ascent of Abruzzi by team members ostensibly with Renato Casarotto. Both suffered frostbitten fingers on the descent.

Date	Names	Nationality	Route	Comments
5th July	Gianni Calcagno Tullio Vidoni Soro Dorotei Martino Moretti Josef Rakoncaj Benoît Chamoux	Italian Italian Italian Italian Czech French	Abruzzi Ridge	An efficient ascent of the Abruzzi by the Italian Quota 8000 expedition attempting all fourteen 8000-metre peaks. Led by Agostino Da Polenza. Josef Rakoncaj became the first person to climb K2 twice, the first time by the North Ridge in 1983; and Benoît Chamoux made an amazing twenty-three-hour solo ascent.
5th July	Beda Furster Rolf Zemp	Swiss Swiss	Abruzzi Ridge	Breakaway couple from Karl Herrligkoffer's international expedition, originally climbing with Kukuczka and Piotrowski on the Central Ridge of the South Face.

		Route	Comments
8th July	Jerzy Kukuczka Tadeusz Piotrowski	Polish Polish	South Face Central Rib	A major new route by a two-man team in very good style, marred by the death of Piotrowski on the descent.
3rd August	Jang Bong Wan Kim Chang Sun Jang Byong Ho	South Korean South Korean South Korean	Abruzzi Ridge	An ascent of the Abruzzi by a large traditional fixed-rope expedition with oxygen, led by Kim Byong Joon
3rd August	Wojciech Wröz Przemyslaw Piasecki Peter Bozik	Polish Polish Czech	South-South-West Ridge	First ascent of the "Magic Line" by Polish expedition led by Janusz Majer. The South-South-West Ridge and the North-West Ridge were the last great problems of K2.

		Route	Comments
4th August	Willi Bauer Alfred Imitzer	Austrian Austrian	Abruzzi Ridge	Alfred Imitzer was the leader of the seven-man Austrian Guides expedition. He and Bauer reached the summit at the second attempt after a day's rest at Camp 4, and were subsequently trapped at Camp 4 in the storm.
4th August	Alan Rouse	British	Abruzzi Ridge	First British ascent of K2.
4th August	Kurt Diemberger Julie Tullis	Austrian British	Abruzzi Ridge	An ascent by the veteran film team from the Quota 8000 expedition. The couple were forced to bivouac below the summit following a fall by Julie Tullis and were subsequently trapped at Camp 4.

Appendix Two

1986, The Tragedies

21st June Two members of the American expedition to the South-South-West Ridge from Portland, Oregon, John Smolich (leader) and Alan Pennington, were killed in a colossal avalanche from just above the Negrotto Col. Pennington's body was recovered and buried at the Gilkey memorial.

24th June Maurice and Liliane Barrard disappeared on the descent of the Abruzzi Ridge after a successful ascent. Liliane's body was found at the foot of the mountain and buried at the Gilkey memorial but the precise circumstances of their deaths are unknown.

10th July Tadeusz Piotrowski fell to his death on the descent of the Abruzzi Ridge after a successful ascent of the Central Rib of the South Face. The accident was caused by the loss of both crampons, but extreme exhaustion and dehydration must have been contributory factors. Piotrowski was the doyen of Polish winter climbing, with first ascents in Poland, the Alps, Hindu Kush and Himalaya to his name.

16th July   Renato Casarotto died in a crevasse fall only minutes from safety after his last unsuccessful attempt to solo the South-South-West Ridge. Casarotto was one of the world's foremost solo mountaineers with first ascents in the Alps, Andes, Patagonia, and Karakoram.

3rd–4th August   Wojciech Wröz died during the night after an epic ascent of the South-South-West Ridge. It would appear that he abseiled off the end of a fixed rope on the upper slopes of the Abruzzi. Wröz had previously climbed Kangchenjunga South (1978) and Yalung Kang (1984) and had twice reached 8000 metres on K2 in 1976 and 1982.

4th August	Mohammed Ali, Sirdar of the South Koreans' high-altitude porters, was killed by stonefall below Camp 1 on the Abruzzi Ridge.
7th August	Julie Tullis died in her sleep after her descent from the summit and enforced bivouac at Camp 4. Julie made the first British female ascent of Broad Peak with Kurt Diemberger in 1984 and had twice attempted K2. She and Diemberger had produced several climbing documentary films in Britain and Europe.
10th August	Two Austrians, Alfred Imitzer and Hannes Wieser, died as they tried to descend from Camp 4 during a break in the storm. Al Rouse was left delirious in his tent at Camp 4 and is presumed to have died on the same day, as is Dobroslawa "Mrufka" Wolf who disappeared on fixed ropes below Camp 3. All were experienced climbers. Rouse had previously climbed Broad Peak, Jannu, Nuptse and the first ascent of Kongur in China.

Appendix Three

An Interview with Willi Bauer

THE day after Willi Bauer and Kurt Diemberger returned to Base Camp, Bauer was interviewed in German by Krystyna Palmowska. The full text of the interview was published in Polish in the magazine *Perspekty Wach* on 2nd November 1986. These extracts in English are therefore at a third remove of language. The original interview was given when Bauer was still exhausted and incoherent. It should be remembered, too, that for Krystyna the death of Mrufka was naturally uppermost in her mind and Bauer, equally understandably, would be trying to give Krystyna the best possible impression of her fellow climber's last days.

K.P.   Why didn't anyone follow the Koreans that day?

W.B.   We needed a day of rest, and the others were probably waiting for the route to be cleared.

We started on 4th August. Alan first, then Mrufka, then Alfred and Diemberger, and Tullis. Hans and I waited till seven o'clock. At seven or 7.15 I started off and reached Hans. It appeared that he had wet gloves, and was going back to the camp. Soon afterwards I overtook Diemberger and reached Alfred. Alfred hadn't anything to drink. I gave him a drink and he recovered some strength. Afterwards I reached Mrufka, who couldn't keep up with Alan, but she desperately wanted to keep climbing. Somewhere above the Ice Traverse I reached Alan. Alan said that it was good that someone could help break trail. Afterwards Alfred overtook Alan. At about 3.30 p.m. I was near the summit. I waited for Alfred and together we went to the top. While we were on the summit we realised that the weather was deteriorating. Soon afterwards we went down and we met Alan. Alan was about fifteen or twenty minutes from the top. Lower down was Mrufka. I told her to go back because it was late and the weather was getting worse. She refused and carried on, but when Alan came he managed to persuade her to go down. Then I met Diemberger.

K.P.   How far from the summit was this?

W.B.   About 150 metres. Diemberger wanted to bivouac, and I told him it might be possible near the sérac. We went further down. I turned, and Mrufka and Alan were climbing down too. Alfred and I reached Camp 4 at about six p.m. Mrufka and Alan arrived about half an hour or an hour later, but Diemberger didn't arrive.

K.P.   Did he bivouac?

W.B.   Yes. They had fallen, but had managed to stop and made a bivouac. When Diemberger and Tullis arrived, they were completely exhausted and frostbitten. Then the disasters began. We took Julie into our tent and we tried to save her. Diemberger slept in his tent. Julie became strong enough to go back to their tent. Then the next disaster occurred. Diemberger had become buried in their tent under the snow. He couldn't get out. Julie was calling for help. I managed to pull her out through the sleeve of the tent. She hardly had any clothes on and had terrible frostbite. She stayed with us and the next morning, died.

The storm did not stop, and to get out of the tent was impossible. The top part of the tent frame was broken, and there was less and less space. We stayed at that level for three days, and our chances of survival grew smaller.

K.P. It was more than three days . . .

W.B. The gas was finished, the food was finished, and we hadn't anything to melt the snow with. It wasn't until 10th August that I decided to go down. The weather didn't give us much chance. Then Mrufka appeared near me carrying her gear. Diemberger also joined us. Alan was asleep, but was talking about melting water in his sleeping bag. Alfred and Hans were suffering badly from the altitude, and had lost their sense of balance. Mrufka and I tried to take them down. Alfred fell deeply into the snow, and tried with the last of his strength to get up. He tried to get up, but he was suffering from blindness, and was also losing his mind. After a while he stopped trying to get up. Hans was very apathetic. He took off his gloves to show me his frostbitten hands. Then Mrufka came with Diemberger and we started going down. It was impossible to see anything. We had to go down blindly, following our noses, towards the sérac, where there was a little bridge. Diemberger came last. Mrufka was helping me to break trail, and she helped me when I fell into the snow. It was really fantastic. We managed to reach Camp 3 at 7300 metres. But the camp wasn't there any more. The tents had been swept away by the wind.

Diemberger joined us and we went down together. We found the sérac. We did very well then. For me the problem was solved then, because below this there were fixed ropes. We went on down the ropes, and I was pulling the ropes out of the snow. Mrufka had a problem with her descendeur. This was why she needed more time to get down. We reached the Koreans' Camp 2. There I found some gas.

K.P. What time was that?

W.B. It was about eight or nine.

K.P. What time did you leave Camp 4?

W.B. About one or two. It was very heavy going, trying to stop Alfred and Hans falling down the crevasses, and I had to keep holding their legs. From Camp 3 it could have been about seven.

K.P. So late? Did you need only an hour?

W.B. Yes. I didn't use the descendeur. I was going down by my hands using a karabiner. I just wanted to get down as quickly as possible.

K.P. Was it dark then?

W.B. Yes, it was dark at Camp 3.

K.P.	And when did you see Mrufka for the last time?
W.B.	When I was going down the ladder, I saw Mrufka and Diemberger at the top of the Black Pyramid.
K.P.	Was it dark then? Because Diemberger said it was about four or five.
W.B.	No, it's difficult to say what time it was, but it was definitely dark. At about one a.m. Diemberger came. I asked him where Mrufka was. He said, "Don't worry, Mrufka has a problem with her descendeur. She will probably go to Wanda's tent."

But dawn came, and Mrufka was not there. I told Diemberger that we should wait, and that Mrufka would probably come at noon. But she didn't come, and we started going down. We presumed that Mrufka had a sleeping bag in her rucksack, and we assumed that she was sleeping in Wanda's tent, trying to recover some strength. I helped Diemberger through House's Chimney, and then I went down to Base Camp to call for help.

K.P.   You arrived here on 11th August at seven p.m. Is there any possibility that Mrufka . . .

W.B.   She must have made some mistake, because she was strong. When I was telling her "Mrufka, do this" or "Do that", there were no problems.

K.P.   Is it possible that she died from exhaustion on the fixed ropes?

W.B.   In my opinion, it is possible that she tripped over her crampons, and fell off when she wasn't tied onto the fixed ropes. Or it's possible she made a mistake abseiling. She couldn't use her hands because she had frostbite.

K.P.   What sort of condition was she in? Both of you had quite serious frostbite.

W.B.   All of us were very tired and exhausted, there's no doubt, but she was always ready to break trail, and she was following right behind me. Once she was even breaking trail by herself. She had amazing determination to get down. She was very happy when we found the sérac again under Camp 3.

K.P.	Was she strong and determined?
W.B.	Yes, there must have been some mistake.
K.P.	Tell me, what sort of person was she in those horrible days at Camp 4?
W.B.	She was the strongest of all of us. When help was needed to dig out the tents, Mrufka was always outside. Alan was lying down and Diemberger was lying down. It was just Mrufka and me. Outside it was terribly windy and we had white hands.
K.P.	Alan was the first to reach the summit, but when it came to a matter of survival . . .
W.B.	Yes, perhaps Mrufka made a mistake going just behind Alan. She was incredibly determined to reach the top. Later, she cried in her tent because she hadn't made it to the top. She hadn't much further to go, and I told her, "Mrufka, be happy that we're alive."
K.P.	Can you tell me why they waited for so long?
W.B.	They should have followed the Koreans. They made a bivouac 200

metres below Camp 4. I don't really know. The weather was fine. I think that everyone, Diemberger and Alan, were waiting for everything to be just right. I wanted to go the next day, after the Koreans. I was okay. But it wasn't clear whether the Koreans had managed to break trail on the final stretch, even with oxygen.

K.P. In your case it was different, because you had tried already on 2nd August.

W.B. If you have had an unsuccessful attempt, it is difficult to summon up enough strength for another summit bid.

K.P. Tell me one thing more. During the six days at Camp 4, did you try to get down earlier?

W.B. Three times I tried to get down, but there was always something. Either it was too late, because it was in the evening when the chance came on 4th or 5th, or there was too much snow and we wouldn't make it.

K.P. Who was saying so?

W.B. Hans, Alfred and Alan.

K.P.	Were your tents near each other?
W.B.	Yes, quite near. Mrufka could understand me better, because their tent was facing against the wind. She was always ready to go down.
K.P.	Did you want to go down?
W.B.	Yes, we'd decided to go down all together, otherwise we wouldn't go.
K.P.	This was a mistake.
W.B.	It was a mistake that I didn't argue with. I was calm. I was thinking, and I believed that everyone else could be right, and this was my mistake. I should have opposed it much earlier, but we were friends, and we didn't want to quarrel.
K.P.	Oh yes, and what about Alan?
W.B.	Alan was in his tent. When we were leaving, he said that he was not going, and that he would melt some water in his sleeping bag, even though there was no gas.
K.P.	Wasn't he sane any more?
W.B.	Everything was so slow-moving when we had no water. Everyone had white hands, proving that the blood was not circulating. The worst thing was that we'd been

lying for so long that we had trouble keeping our balance.

K.P.   Thank you very much, Willi.

W.B.   It is difficult to say when I have met such a super girl, and she died.

Appendix Four

The First Woman's Ascent of K2
Wanda Rutkiewicz

IN 1986 I participated in the small French expedition with Maurice Barrard as leader, his wife, Liliane, and Michel Parmentier. I had met the Barrards the year before on Broad Peak and for me it was an enjoyable meeting and an important one, for they changed a lot of my thinking about climbing in high mountains. I was impressed with their style, almost alpine-style, and being a very small party had a romantic air to it. So I was very happy to accompany them to K2.

It would be my third attempt on that mountain. On the first, in 1982, I led a Polish-French women's expedition. In 1984 I was also in an all-women team. I was very familiar with the route up to 7350 metres, the level of our previous Camp 3 on the Abruzzi Ridge. But now our style was to be different. We didn't have oxygen or fixed ropes and we didn't want to establish many camps. We were the first expedition on the Abruzzi Ridge that year, so we did not have the benefit of other people's trail-breaking, camps or fixed ropes which all assisted later expeditions.

We reached Base Camp on 22nd May. Only Renato Casarotto, his wife Goretta, and the two Basques were there then. A month later there were nine expeditions at Base Camp. The biggest and richest was the South Korean expedition with its oxygen bottles and high-altitude porters. They brought a little comfort into our Base Camp lives as we drank sixteen different types of Korean tea with them and watched videos of James Bond and *Ninja Two*. The Koreans put a line of fixed ropes from Advance Base up to the top of the Black Pyramid, a distance of more than 2000 metres. It made the way easier not only for them, but also for descending climbers of other expeditions, and helped the last mixed group climbing the summit at the beginning of August.

But in May and June there was not yet

any new fixed rope on the route. Maurice and Liliane avoided using old fixed ropes from previous seasons, except on the most difficult places such as at House's Chimney. They were against fixed high camps, too. Their view was that it is better to carry very light-weight bivouac gear and be free to stop when and where we wanted, rather than be tied to moving between fixed camps. We only established two camps during our acclimatisation period and during the summit bid we used only the first of these. After that we carried just our bivouac gear.

This kind of climbing was new to me, but very interesting. I was not apprehensive, being confident that what Liliane could do, I could do also. I should have enjoyed climbing as a pair with Liliane because I was not getting on at all well with Michel, but she and Maurice were a good team, on the mountain as well as in life, so there was no question of splitting them. I would just have to share my tent with Michel.

On 25th May the others put up one tent for our Camp 1 at 6200 metres, 200 metres higher than the usual spot for Camp 1. At the time I was in Base Camp with a high fever and tonsilitis, being attended to by the British team doctor. But on the 31st I was ready to join my French partners. We equipped our Camp 1 and on 2nd June started up new ground. Bad weather stopped us at the foot of House's Chimney, so we made a bivouac there. The next day, during very strong winds, we reached a height of about 7000 metres and established our Camp 2, again 200 metres higher than the usual Camp 2 site. We spent a night there and came back down to Base Camp next day.

On 8th June we climbed up from Base Camp, sleeping at Advance Base, Camp 1 and Camp 2. Very bad and windy weather prevented us getting any higher. We spent a second night at Camp 2, hoping the weather would change. The others were already thinking about a summit bid, but it was too early for me to feel completely acclimatised. However, bad weather solved the problem for all of us and we retreated to Base Camp again on 12th June.

Here we prepared for the summit attempt we should be making next time we went up the mountain. During these rest days the relationship between Michel and me was getting so bad that I borrowed a light two-person tent from the British so that I could bivouac separately. Three tents for four people sounds a bit much, but the extra weight in my sack was the price of independence.

We left for our summit attempt on 18th June, spending the first night at Camp 1, then missing out Camp 2, and instead making a bivouac at about 7100 metres on the ridge of the Black Pyramid, where we cached some gear to lighten our sacks. We passed the usual Camp 3 site at 7350 metres and bivouacked at 7700 metres under the big barrier of the overhanging sérac in a conveniently level patch of snow which was only a little dangerous. Next day we should have been making our last bivouac before the summit, but unfortunately we got no higher than 7900 metres.

This was partly due to very high winds, but we also lost time on the sérac barrier above our bivouac. Michel went first up a steep slope and in doing so collapsed a snow bridge above a crevasse, making it dangerous for the rest of us to follow without a rope, and he had gone on with the only one. Finding a way round was laborious and our variation ended in a difficult overhang about three metres high. The snow was soft and I eventually climbed it with the help of Maurice reaching down from above to give me a hand. It was the first time I'd climbed an overhang at this altitude! But the delay it caused meant that we had no chance of reaching the summit next day and would have to make a further bivouac at 8300 metres.

By now our loads were completely reduced. We didn't carry any sleeping bags or rope, we had only one stove and only one small tent. It made soloing the Bottleneck and the rock traverse above much easier. There were no fixed ropes up there. But the biggest problem was above —very deep snow. We took turns at breaking trail at first, but Michel led for the last 150 metres as we were too slow for him. He found a small rock platform for the bivouac and we spent the night there at about 8300 metres without sleeping bags in a very bad condition, all four squeezed into one small tent.

Next morning, the sixth day of our ascent, the weather was good, sunny, cloudless and there were no strong winds. This day was my day. I had got a new surge of power after the bivouac. We set out at about seven or 7.30. I brought up the rear and when I caught up with my French partners I found that they had decided to rest. "Now we will rest here for a couple of hours and cook something," I remember Maurice saying. It was so strange to be hanging about cooking so near the summit. Afterwards I wondered if I had been hallucinating. After all, who had carried the stove for the last 300 metres? But it was true. Later climbers found the remains of our One Minute Soup.

I didn't want to stay such a long time there drinking soup. I was in a hurry. The summit was beckoning. So I left the others and started out on my own. They asked why I was going to the right. The logical route seemed to be straight ahead. But I remembered an account by the Swiss who were on the mountain last year. They found an easier variant by going right first and afterwards to the left. Much easier.

At about 10.15 a.m. I reached the summit. It was my third attempt. I was excited and happy, happy to be alone there, because I could express my enormous gratitude. I knelt and prayed. I said a big thank you for the summit, for good weather, and for feeling good. And now I was looking forward to greeting my partners. But I had to wait about an hour. After the first moments of great happiness I started to grow impatient. I had to do something. I climbed down a little onto the rocks of the North Face where I left a plastic bag with a message in it containing my name, the date, the time and the words "First Woman's Ascent". Below, I wrote Liliane's name, but left the time for when she arrived. (In the event I forgot to add it). I added a small Polish flag, anchored the bag and climbed back to the top again, but still nobody had come. So I descended a little on the North-East side and collected about a kilo of small stones as souvenirs. Then I returned to the summit and descended a little down the South Face. I could see two climbers about a hundred metres below, not our route, and wondered whom they might be. Later I learnt they were the Basque pair. A few minutes later I saw my French friends, Liliane and Maurice Barrard and Michel Parmentier, following in my tracks. We spent an hour on the summit taking photographs. Liliane was really happy. "I have never had such good weather on any other of my summits," she told me. At noon we began our descent. We didn't meet the Basques because they climbed a different route.

A few hours later we reached our bivouac at 8300 metres and while we rested Maurice and Michel decided we should stay there for the night. I was surprised, but not unhappy. "I don't need to go down today," I thought. I was tired, but not exhausted. The weather was still good and I was not worried. But I should have been. One should remain at that altitude as short a time as possible. I didn't know in the sunshine that death was following us down. I didn't see any signals of something wrong.

I had a bad night. Perhaps the others did too, but nobody said so. It was not too cold inside the tent, but I could not rest and altitude seemed to accentuate my antipathy to Michel. In the end I took two and a half sleeping tablets. Then it was easier. The Barrards didn't move much and didn't speak.

The next morning was still beautiful. Michel left first. I concentrated on keeping my balance and staying upright after so much Mogadon. I was very sleepy, but conscious. The descent would wake me up! For I realised I would now have to fight for my life as I descended the rock traverse and the Bottleneck solo. I was concentrating on myself because I knew that nobody else could help me at that height unroped. So I didn't notice that the Barrards were more tired than usual. We didn't speak much as we prepared our slow descent. I didn't wait for them and knew they could help each other. I had to look out for myself.

After the difficult traverse the snow of the Bottleneck was easier going. The Basques had left their bivouac at the bottom of the Bottleneck and I followed in their tracks and those of Michel. Before reaching the sérac barrier I looked back. I saw two people in the Bottleneck, 300 metres above. The larger figure was just above the smaller one. I was surprised that they were going so slowly, but at least they had made the traverse, and though the Bottleneck was steep it was not too difficult because there was plenty of snow. That was the last time I saw the Barrards alive.

As I descended through the sérac barrier the weather deteriorated. I could barely see where I was going but fortunately the tracks of Michel and the Basques were quite fresh and they led me to the bivouac at 7700 metres. From here the summit is not visible. There were Italian and French climbers at the bivouac, their Camp 3, and we discussed what to do about the Barrards. But with visibility at zero we could do nothing. We assumed they still had the tent and could spend the night in that. Next morning, the 25th, the weather was still bad. We waited until noon but nobody appeared. It was clear now that something had happened.

Michel decided to wait for the Barrards and urged everyone else to go down, including the French climber Benoît Chamoux and myself. "You should go down with the Italians and the Basques," he told me. "We don't have enough gas for more to stay." So we went. I decided to climb down to our Camp 2 at 7000 metres and wait there for the others. I hoped I would be able to make walkie-talkie contact. Going down I lost contact with the Italians in front. Visibility was nil and new snow quickly covered their tracks. The wind was very strong. The Italians didn't wait for me because they had seen me carrying a tent and thought I would be bivouacking. They couldn't know that it was the tent I had borrowed from the British which I was trying to bring back to them. I tried to hold onto the tent in the high wind, but in wrestling with it I lost my gloves and I had to let the tent go. It just went flying off somewhere. I was completely alone. I had to concentrate very hard to find my way on that snowslope. Then I found the Basques and soon we heard the Italians. Suddenly we saw the ski sticks which marked the start of the fixed ropes. The storm over the Black Pyramid was growing stronger by the minute. Hunting for our gear cache, I told the Basques not to wait for me, and was left alone again. I couldn't find the cache which contained the walkie-talkie, and gave up the search as I was nearly at my limit. In the evening I reached the camp at 7000 metres. It had been the worst day I had had on K2. But I had been lucky. The biggest bit of luck was to find the old fixed ropes which I had been afraid to use on the way up.

Camp 2 was fully equipped and I could have sat out the storm there, but I decided to continue down on the 27th. My hands were frostbitten, but I didn't take the spare gloves belonging to the Barrards. I put socks on my hands instead. Sometime, I told myself, they will be down. But at other times I thought perhaps I was the only one of our team left alive. Between the Koreans' Camp 1 and Advance Base I met Benoît Chamoux who was going up to meet Michel. He was surprised to see me alive because at Base Camp people were getting concerned that I was missing, for they had no radio contact with me, only with Michel. Next I met the Polish climbers, Wojciech Wröz and Przemyslaw Piasecki, who had come up to look for me. After three days alone on the mountain in some terrible weather it was marvellous to meet people again. I reached Advance Base on the 27th, the same day as Michel. Here, while enjoying the hospitality of the Koreans, I received some medical attention for my frostbitten hands from the American doctor, Steve Boyer, who had come up to meet us. We arrived back at Base Camp on 28th June.

But Liliane and Maurice Barrard never arrived. A month later Liliane's body was found at the foot of the mountain. Maurice's body was never found. We buried Liliane at the Gilkey memorial and I asked Michael Messner to make a memorial plaque for her and to add Maurice's name. Perhaps somebody on a future expedition will find his body and bury him with Liliane.

How did the Barrards die? Possibly part of the summit sérac broke off and hit them as they climbed down in the Bottleneck. Perhaps the one behind, Maurice, was exhausted and fell, taking Liliane with him. Perhaps they lost their way on the big snowslopes below the Bottleneck during the white-out and were avalanched down the South Face. I'm sure, too, we stayed too long at altitude. The cooking on the summit day, the slow descent from the bivouac at 8300 metres both showed that the Barrards were more exhausted than Michel and I realised. That's how accidents happen.

I can feel no pleasure at having reached the summit of K2. For a long time I couldn't write about the tragedies, or the successes. I didn't sell pictures or articles to the media on my return. I had lost too many friends in 1986—Liliane and Maurice Barrard, Tadeusz Piotrowski, Renato Casarotto, Julie Tullis, Alan Rouse, Hannes Wieser, Alfred Imitzer, and my two best Polish friends, Wojciech Wröz and Dobroslawa Miodowicz-Wolf. When my film and my book are ready, they will be their memorial.

Wanda Rutkiewicz
Pokhara, January 1987
Warsaw, March 1987

Appendix Five

Benoît Chamoux's Account of his Rapid Ascents

ON 4th June, after ten very hard days on the move, in which I was laid low by fever and every illness on earth, we set up our Base Camp at the foot of K2 at an altitude of 5100 metres. Thanks to an initial period of relatively good weather, we were able to acclimatise as we set up the first camp on our initial route, the South-South-West Arête of K2.

Camp 1 at 5700 metres, Camp 2 at 6350 metres: an American team were also taking this route. So, curbing our efforts on K2, we decided to concentrate first on climbing Broad Peak, and on 15th June we set up a camp at 6300 metres.

In the afternoon of the 19th, making the most of an initial period of good weather, I left Base Camp, in order to bivouac at the foot of Broad Peak at an altitude of 4900 metres. After a few hours' sleep, I began my climb at midnight by the light of the lamp on my helmet. At this point the mountain was also lit by the moon, making my progress easier.

After one hour and forty-five minutes' climbing, I reached Camp 1 at 5700 metres, where I took a few minutes' welcome rest and broke into the provisions for the first time. I had a flask and a little food in my rucksack. It took me another one hour and forty-five minutes to get to Camp 2, which had been set up five days earlier at 6350 metres. I stopped here for half an hour, melted some snow on the stove, drank a lot to rehydrate myself, ate, and then continued my climb up to Camp 3 at 7100 metres. Half way there the sun came out. It took me three hard hours to reach the camp. I left again at 08.00 hours, after an hour's break to stock up for the last time, before setting off for the summit, towering a thousand metres above me. At 13.00 hours I reached the pass between the two main summits at 7800 metres and caught up with my Quota 8000 companions who had left Camp 3 that morning. The snow, deep in places, had slowed down their progress. I climbed up the rocks and through the snow of the final long arête, where a wind was blowing from Sinkiang. At 16.00 hours I reached the main summit of Broad Peak, towering at an altitude of 8047 metres. The weather was marvellous. Before deciding to begin the descent I spent an hour gazing round in delight at the never-ending panorama of the Himalayan peaks. At 23.00 hours I reached my bivouac at the foot of the mountain some 3147 metres below. During the day the face was swept away by an avalanche coming from the séracs.

The next day I returned to Base Camp to receive some bad news. Two Americans had been killed on the South-South-West Spur route of K2 in an avalanche from Negrotto Col. Luckily the three members of our team who were taking this route to set up Camp 3 at 6800 metres were safe not many metres above the avalanche point. These objective dangers and the unchanging weather persuaded us to attempt a rapid ascent of K2 by the Abruzzi Ridge. On 22nd June four of us set off in the night and in two days, in alpine-style, reached an altitude of 7600 metres, where we made our second bivouac. The storm which then forced us to return to Base Camp would be partly responsible for the disappearance of the Barrards on the same route. A period of unsettled weather trapped us at Base Camp.

On 4th July, I left Base Camp and reached the foot of the Abruzzi Ridge at 5300 metres. At 18.00 hours after a meal of plain rice, I began climbing the first snow-covered slopes. It was dark by the time I arrived at Camp 1 at 6200 metres at 20.00 hours. I had my first very light snack, then continued up the rock spur. It was a very dark night. I could sometimes see along the route the lights of Base Camp a few kilometres below. A capricious wind was blowing around my ears all through the night. By the light of my helmet I got through House's Chimney. At 22.30 hours I got into the tent at Camp 2 at 6700 metres, already feeling those four hours of effort. I had an hour's rest before going back to melt some snow and drink from my flask, which was full of boiling liquid to help me combat the cold wind over those final spur rises. The rocky climb grew more unpleasant and difficult. In the daylight I got over the sérac ridge which leads up to the higher slopes. It was 07.00 hours when I reached the end of the long slope to arrive at the camp at 7600 metres at the foot of the Shoulder.

After thirty minutes' rest I left my rucksack and continued the climb. The wind had fallen and the sun on that east side was becoming very hot. As on Broad Peak, my Quota 8000 companions had set off about two hours earlier to climb the final thousand metres of the mountain. From the top of the Shoulder I could see them at the other end of the huge false plateau which leads to the foot of the Bottleneck, a dangerous passage under the last séracs of K2. The sun deserted me through this notorious passage, and it was with great difficulty that I climbed the slopes of the world's second highest mountain.

8611 metres, a twenty-three-hour climb, and I was finally at the top of the marvellous pyramid of rock and ice. It was 17.00 hours. I enjoyed the view at the summit for thirty minutes, but then I had to plunge back into the shaded abyss, leaving the heat and the ecstasy of the summit and trying not to make any mistakes on the way down. In the night I rejoined my companions at the Camp at 7600 metres for a short night of sleep. The next morning I continued my descent to Base Camp, where I arrived without incident to share lunch with our team mates below.

For each of these two rapid climbs, a new style of Himalayan performance, I followed over the five days preceding my departure a special diet aimed at furthering performance. On the one hand it sorts out the "combination of food"—that means dividing up the proteins, fats and glucose in each meal, each in turn serving as a base. On the other hand it spreads out the various foods, taking into account their "profitability" as far as the body and effort are concerned. Nevertheless I must add that I could not eat during the final phase of the climb, the strenuousness of effort combined with the effects of the altitude and of a rapid climb having a harmful effect on the digestive process.

Benoît Chamoux

Appendix Six

A Stranger on the Shoulder

IN *Mountain* no. 112 I came upon a surprising reference:

"In preparation for the 1988 Yugoslav K2 Expedition, Tomo Cesen, after a fast solo ascent of Broad Peak, made an interesting reconnaissance of K2. He climbed the South-South-East Spur to its junction with the Abruzzi Spur at 7800 metres on 3rd-4th August. This is the line explored by Alan Rouse and Roger Baxter-Jones in 1983."

I thought there must be some mistake with the dates and perhaps it was 3rd-4th *July*, and did not give the matter much thought, apart from marvelling that the event could have seemingly escaped everyone's attention. But then it was confirmed by H. Adams Carter. How on earth could someone have blithely soloed up to the Shoulder, presumably to within metres of Camp 4, and soloed down the Abruzzi without anyone knowing? I just couldn't understand. That the ascent was almost certainly, like Al's on the Abruzzi, an illicit attempt on the summit might explain why he had avoided the Strip. But surely the Koreans or Peter and Przemyslaw would have seen him at some point? Later in a report to the *American Alpine Journal* I read that Tomo Cesen had started on the afternoon of 3rd August and reached the Shoulder seventeen hours later. He had gone a hundred metres up the Shoulder before being turned back by "strong wind and snowfall". Assuming that "afternoon" means, say two p.m., he would have arrived on the Shoulder at seven a.m. the next morning. It is conceivable that he started his descent before either the Poles or Koreans. But it is interesting that he mentions strong wind and snowfall which would seem to indicate a much later arrival on the Shoulder, in which case the Poles and Koreans would have been ahead of him. It is possible that he overtook them in the dark or that, in their exhaustion, they simply forgot to mention that they had seen him.

The significant thing for me, of course, was his mention of strong winds and snowfall, thus confirming that the storm had broken on the 4th. As Willi Bauer also mentions in his interview with Krystyna that he urged Mrufka to turn back "because it was late and the weather was getting worse", and also that on the summit "we realised that the weather was deteriorating", it is clear to me that, unless the seven climbers' minds were so totally blinkered by their desire for the summit that they simply didn't notice, they *must* have known that the weather was breaking and decided to chance their arm. It was a race against time that, sadly, they lost. I simply cannot believe that the warning signs that were so obvious at Base Camp could have failed to register higher up: each fine weather spell had ended in the same way and on this occasion there was even less reason to assume it would continue.

GUIDE
TO THE COLOUR CODING
OF
ULVERSCROFT BOOKS

Many of our readers have written to us expressing their appreciation for the way in which our colour coding has assisted them in selecting the Ulverscroft books of their choice. To remind everyone of our colour coding— this is as follows:

BLACK COVERS
Mysteries

*

BLUE COVERS
Romances

*

RED COVERS
Adventure Suspense and General Fiction

*

ORANGE COVERS
Westerns

*

GREEN COVERS
Non-Fiction

NON-FICTION TITLES
in the
Ulverscroft Large Print Series

MYSTERY TITLES
in the
Ulverscroft Large Print Series

Henrietta Who?	*Catherine Aird*
Slight Mourning	*Catherine Aird*
The China Governess	*Margery Allingham*
Coroner's Pidgin	*Margery Allingham*
Crime at Black Dudley	*Margery Allingham*
Look to the Lady	*Margery Allingham*
More Work for the Undertaker	
	Margery Allingham
Death in the Channel	*J. R. L. Anderson*
Death in the City	*J. R. L. Anderson*
Death on the Rocks	*J. R. L. Anderson*
A Sprig of Sea Lavender	*J. R. L. Anderson*
Death of a Poison-Tongue	*Josephine Bell*
Murder Adrift	*George Bellairs*
Strangers Among the Dead	*George Bellairs*
The Case of the Abominable Snowman	
	Nicholas Blake
The Widow's Cruise	*Nicholas Blake*
The Brides of Friedberg	*Gwendoline Butler*
Murder By Proxy	*Harry Carmichael*
Post Mortem	*Harry Carmichael*
Suicide Clause	*Harry Carmichael*
After the Funeral	*Agatha Christie*
The Body in the Library	*Agatha Christie*

K 2 and the Central Karakoram